FROG HOLLOW

HartfordBooks

HartfordBooks is a book series that seeks to
rediscover Hartford's philosophies, people
large and small, history, and culture. The
series is supported by the University of
Hartford, Wesleyan University Press, and
Hartford Foundation for Public Giving.

SUSAN CAMPBELL

Frog Hollow

STORIES FROM AN AMERICAN NEIGHBORHOOD

Wesleyan University Press | Middletown, Connecticut

Wesleyan University Press
Middletown CT 06459
www.wesleyan.edu/wespress
© 2019 Susan Campbell
All rights reserved
Manufactured in the United States of America
Designed by Mindy Basinger Hill
Typeset in Adobe Jenson Pro

This book is part of HartfordBooks,
a series developed through a partnership
of Wesleyan University Press and the
University of Hartford, and supported by
Hartford Foundation for Public Giving.
wesleyan.edu/wespress/hartfordbooks

Library of Congress Cataloging-in-Publication Data

Names: Campbell, Susan, 1959– author.

Title: Frog Hollow: stories from an American neighborhood / Susan Campbell.

Description: Middletown, Connecticut: Wesleyan University Press, 2019. |
Includes bibliographical references and index.

Identifiers: LCCN 2018033857 (print) | LCCN 2018034562 (ebook) |
ISBN 9780819578556 (ebook) | ISBN 9780819576200 (cloth: alk. paper)

Subjects: LCSH: Frog Hollow (Hartford, Conn.)—History—Anecdotes. |
Frog Hollow (Hartford, Conn.)—Social life and customs—Anecdotes. |
Frog Hollow (Hartford, Conn.)—Biography—Anecdotes. | Hartford (Conn.)—
History—Anecdotes. | Hartford (Conn.)—Social life and customs—Anecdotes. |
Hartford (Conn.)—Biography—Anecdotes.

Classification: LCC F104.H3 (ebook) | LCC F104.H3 C27 2019 (print) |
DDC 974.6/3—dc23

LC record available at https://lccn.loc.gov/2018033857

5 4 3 2 1

Title page image: Zion Street at Russ Street. April 6, 1996. Tony DeBonee Collection,
Hartford History Center, Hartford Public Library

Dedication page image: Family portrait of Constance Schiavone

Contents

Author's Note

In 1986 I moved to Connecticut to work for the *Hartford Courant,* America's oldest continuously published newspaper—a phrase that still forms itself as one word in my head, even seven years after leaving that job. At the time, Hartford's better days were behind it, or so I was told. Drug and gang wars held the city by the throat. Schools were struggling. The go-go '80s appeared to be passing the capital city by.

But Hartford was so much more than gangs and crime and troubled schools. I know because I was there, and when I was occasionally asked to give speeches in suburban libraries or small-town schools, invariably someone would raise a hand to ask if I went into the big, scary city every day.

"Only on days I want to be paid," I would answer, thinking I was giving their tremulous concern just the right amount of disdain.

I see now how insufferable I was. The suburbanites whose main contact with Hartford was to drive in for a concert or play, or to commute to work and then rush home at 5 p.m., were only responding to what they thought they knew. Too often, stories of the schools doing incredible things with limited resources or of trailblazers making the capital city awesome got lost, along with history and context that might have helped explain Hartford.

I made my living and my reputation in Hartford, and so I feel obligated to at least try to explain the place. I am not a social scientist or a professional historian. I am, however, a keen observer and a trained interrogator. I do not know how to tell the story of an entire city, so I want to explore one of the neighborhoods I most like.

Toward the end of my decades-long career at the *Courant*, when I would get angry (and that was often), I would stomp out of the paper and head south. North was Asylum Hill, which had too many busy intersections for someone who didn't want to stop for cars but just wanted to stomp off her mad.

South was Frog Hollow, which had a vibe I couldn't define, other than to say the neighborhood gave off the feeling of being multilayered. Something had happened here, and even if I was walking strictly to enjoy a burrito at El Nuevo Sarape or heading to look at produce I didn't recognize at Park Street's El Mercado, I knew as I walked past apartment buildings and bodegas that what I was seeing was only the most recent layer of a thick historical onion.

There were the trash blowing in the street and the junked cars on the roads, but there was also a pregnant sense of . . . something. Something happened here. So here's to peeling back the onion's layers and admitting that we didn't just arrive here. Here's to getting to the story, the real one and not necessarily the one we tell ourselves. To people lost to history who shouldn't be. To giving credit where it's due: generations of people climbing the ladder.

Here's to the messy but always hopeful history of Frog Hollow.

Introduction

Hartford, Connecticut, was established in June 1636, when a group of Boston-based Puritans followed the Reverend Thomas Hooker, a fifty-year-old orator who earlier had fled England under the threat of prosecution. The band of one hundred or so traveled for two weeks toward a Dutch settlement on the banks of the Connecticut River.

The Dutch weren't the first inhabitants of the area. The first recorded residents were the Suckiaug people, a small tribe that somehow managed to score fertile bottom land crisscrossed by heavily traveled trails. That meant trade, and wealth, for the natives. The Dutch eventually left the area for what is now upstate New York. The Suckiaug (there are multiple ways to spell that) assimilated or moved on as well. The English remained, only to be joined eventually by a variety of people, who brought sights, sounds, and smells from around the world.

And so it has gone for Hartford from the beginning, sometimes because newcomers were seeking something better, and sometimes because newcomers were forced out of their homes by famine, flood, or war. This is a lot of ground to cover, historically speaking, and I am going to tell this story the only way I know how, journalistically, with the stories of people.

Hartford, located slightly north of dead center in the state of Connecticut, is a town of just over 123,000, with all the challenges a midsized city can claim. The neighborhood of Frog Hollow is located just to the southwest of dead-center Hartford, next to downtown and grand state buildings. Frog Hollow is thirty-five square blocks laid out over seventeen acres and home to just over 16,000 residents. A marsh gives the neighborhood its name, though subsequent generations once claimed that the "frog" came from the influx of French Canadians who began moving to the hollow in the 1850s to work in the factories. Perfect Sixes—brick apartment buildings that are three stories high, with two units per floor—line the streets with a beautiful functionality that is almost Shakeresque.

Those bricks are good quality. The wooden floors, if they weren't gummed up with a shag carpet in the 1970s, are attractive oak and pine. They stand as monuments to factory owners who wanted their workers to live well so that they could work well.

For most of Hartford's commuters anxious to get to work and then home again, Frog Hollow is trash blowing on the streets and men hanging out on Park Street. The schools are challenged to take in some of Hartford's poorest students and prepare them for success. If you're zipping by and only half paying attention, the place has a rundown feel; but this scrappy little plot of land has a history packed with innovation and technology birthed by wave after wave of immigrants. Frog Hollow has historically been the entry point for families wishing to participate in, and benefit from, the opportunities offered in a city. They've wanted, generation after generation, to have a shot at the American Dream, even before anyone thought to call it that.

We won't agree on a definition for the American Dream. For my generation it included home ownership. Today's Millennials aren't so sure. But James Truslow Adams, a former banker who became a Pulitzer-winning author, came up with a workable definition in his 1931 book *The Epic of America*. Adams wanted to name the book

"The American Dream," but his publishers advised against it. No one, they said, would spend three dollars for a book with "Dream" in the title during the worst of the Depression. Undeterred, Adams used the phrase "American dream" thirty times in the books' pages, and *Epic* became an international bestseller. The American Dream, wrote Adams,

> is that dream of a land in which life should be better and richer and fuller for everyone, with opportunity for each according to ability or achievement. It is a difficult dream for the European upper classes to interpret adequately, and too many of us ourselves have grown weary and mistrustful of it. It is not a dream of motor cars and high wages merely, but a dream of social order in which each man and each woman shall be able to attain to the fullest stature of which they are innately capable, and be recognized by others for what they are, regardless of the fortuitous circumstances of birth or position.[1]

Despite publishers' concerns, the idea was precisely the rallying cry Americans wanted. In his introduction to *Epic*'s 2012 edition, Howard Schneiderman, a Lafayette College professor of sociology, wrote that the book couldn't have been better timed. Its hopeful note resonated with readers, and Adams's "famous metaphorical phrase took off like a rocket."[2] Adams gave them hope. This was America. The possibilities were endless.

The idea still has resonance. Ask any random group about the American Dream, and you'll hear about social mobility and the opportunity to pull one's self up by one's bootstraps, to overcome inexplicable odds, to fashion a life out of one's own vigor. Ask any person on an American street, and you're likely to get a truncated version of Adams's ideal, which includes, inexplicably, a white picket fence (in Frog Hollow that white picket fence would more likely be a knee-high wrought-iron one).[3]

The American Dream has been given its last rites multiple times, but it is never far from our conversations. Recent discussions about what to do (or not) with Syrian refugees referenced the Statue of Liberty, the symbol of this country as a nation of immigrants (discounting the natives who were here in the first place), and those immigrants rising above their earlier stations to Be Somebody. For at least some residents of this country, Emma Lazarus's "Give me your tired, your poor, your huddled masses yearning to breathe free" still means something.

You can learn a lot by taking a deep dive into one American neighborhood, especially if it's one as vital as Frog Hollow, a neighborhood that has served as a petri dish for every important movement in American culture from its inception, from before the streets were paved—even before there were streets. From the beginning, the land was a significant site for original residents who walked Connecticut's inland forests. Later it was home to an influential colonial newspaper and a water well of magical proportions, until it morphed into a formidable manufacturing center that turned out an amazingly varied array of goods, including sewing machines, bicycles, machine tools, and guns. Here immigrants filled their kitchens with the smells of eastern Europe, Italy, and Ireland. Here owners of speakeasies and ham-fisted cops battled for territory. And here an awakening Puerto Rican community moved from a neighborhood church basement to grab a firm hold on the state's political power, all within forty short years.

Perhaps more than anywhere else in Connecticut's capital city, people came to Frog Hollow for the opportunity to learn English, get a job, and one day afford a home for their family. Frog Hollow was the springboard onto which generations of Americans and would-be Americans jumped so that they could land in a better life, however they defined that life. People came to Frog Hollow, and they bounced. The Italians bounced south from Frog Hollow to the town of Wethersfield; the Irish bounced southeast to Glastonbury; African

Three Kings Day, Park Street. January 6, 1997. Tony DeBonee Collection, Hartford History Center, Hartford Public Library

Americans bounced north to Windsor and Bloomfield; and Latinos and Hispanics bounced east to Manchester and East Hartford. People came to Frog Hollow, got their financial legs beneath them, and then moved on and up, trading their urban life for a suburban one. As Adams said, they attained, "to the fullest stature of which they are innately capable," their new station in life, wrought by their own hard work and ability to adapt to a new culture. They pursued the American Dream. But first, they came to a richly cultured, multilayered neighborhood that sat waiting to receive them.

The world has changed, but not that much. People still come to Frog Hollow, and they still want to bounce. If we are looking for America—and the dream defined by Adams—we would do well to start with Frog Hollow.

FROG HOLLOW

1. The Difficult Dream

THE BABCOCKS DIG A WELL AND
LAUNCH A NEWSPAPER

The Babcock family's colonial saltbox house—its steep-pitched roof sloping from a high front to a low back—sat near what is now the intersection of Capitol Avenue and Lafayette Street in Hartford. The wooden house had a central brick chimney, and its front door opened to an entryway, with rooms branching off a central hall.[1] The architecture was simple, sturdy, and fortified with oak timbers that measured sixteen to eighteen inches.[2]

As houses went, it was pretty standard, but the marvel of the property was outdoors. Just after the American Revolution, no one could explain the well on Dolly Welles Babcock's one-hundred-acre farm, but even people passing through town knew about it. Dolly Babcock's well is one of the first recorded stories from the neighborhood's European history, and it illustrates the combination of luck and hard work that built Frog Hollow.

A 1781 visitor described the Babcock well as preternaturally plentiful. When the well was dug, near today's intersection of Park and Washington streets, "the water sprouted up with such amazing velocity" that workers could barely set the stones.[3]

In fact, the gusher came so fast that the men digging the well had to scramble to avoid drowning. Only after they made it out did they realize they had lost more than a few tools in the gushing water. After the water was tamed, logs were cut and hollowed out to fit into one another, end to end. The person who cut and fit the pine logs—perhaps it was Nahum Carter, a Vermont sawyer—did an excellent job.[4] In 1896 excavators unearthed some of the original wooden pipes and found the legend "1796?" carved into them. A law that was passed in May 1797 created a corporation "for the purpose of water into the city of Hartford, by means of subterraneous pipes, and their successors be, and they are hereby incorporated for said purpose, and made a body politic, by the name of The Proprietors of the Hartford Aqueduct," which provided drinking water to Hartford residents who could afford twelve dollars a year per share.[5] The proprietors included one Elisha Babcock, Dolly's husband.

The well was so famous that in 1847 the *Courant* reported that it frequently overflowed from its "perennial springs."[6] When more pipes were dug up in 1908, according to the *Courant*, they were said to have carried water so sweet that it was like the "drops of the morning."

The water company eventually dissolved, but not before it made the Babcocks wealthy.[7] The family did not have to worry—as did fellow Hartford residents—about the source and quality of their water.

While Dolly Babcock and her five children ran the farm, her husband, Elisha, ran a successful newspaper, the *American Mercury*.[8] The first edition appeared on July 12, 1784, a Monday, and ran just four pages, with a half dozen columns per page printed in blisteringly small type. As was the custom for newspapers of that era, scant local news graced the paper and the national and international news that did exist was often days old. Traveling at the speed of horse and boat, news of an event in Washington easily took five days to reach the pages of the *Mercury*.

The *Mercury* prospectus promised to "furnish a useful and elegant entertainment for the different classes" of customers."[9] In fact, early American newspapers weren't news so much as reprinted gossip, letters from afar, and overheard tavern conversations. Most were, journalistically, little more than the throwaway, ad-heavy publications available at supermarket checkouts today, according to *Older Than the Nation: The Story of the Hartford Courant*, a 1964 book by John Bard McNulty. News wasn't a publisher's bread and butter anyway. The bills were paid by other print jobs taken on, or by selling notions at the publisher's print shop. The idea of news judgment—or placing news in a newspaper according to its importance—was light-years away. The *Courant* ran the Declaration of Independence on page two, "in keeping with the printing custom of the times that arranged the news approximately in the order in which it arrived at the printing office," wrote McNulty.[10]

The *Mercury* and the *Courant* were two of the 180 newspapers that dotted the early American landscape. All told, the papers had a combined circulation of roughly twelve million and were vital to forming a sense of community.[11] Newspapers were the connective tissue between colonists and among the early Americans. Then as today they created a sense of place. They provided information, succor, and a sense of belonging. James Parker, of the eighteenth-century New Haven–based newspaper the *Connecticut Gazette*, wrote: "It is no wonder that a darling so carefully guarded and powerfully supported, should sometimes grow wanton and luxurious, and misuse an indulgence granted it, merely to preserve its just freedom inviolate: It has been tho't safer to suffer it to go beyond the bounds that might strictly be justified by reason."[12]

But early American newspapers did not have long shelf lives, even in a city as hyperliterate and news-hungry as Hartford. Of the eight newspapers started in the capital city in the 1780s, only two, including the *Mercury*, were still publishing twenty years later.

The *Mercury* did not survive by being tepid. Babcock's paper was outspoken enough to offend a Federalist member of the clergy in Litchfield, Conn. In 1806 the Reverend Dan Huntington sued Babcock for "willful falsehood." Despite multiple witnesses who testified in his favor, Babcock was found guilty and fined one thousand dollars. He pouted in the *Mercury*, "We live in a conquered country."

Furthermore, Babcock wrote, anxious to guard the freedom of the press (all spellings are his): "It does not hurt character nor feelings nor the Law to declare of certain republican clergy-men that they are ideots and apastates, nor to charge other republicans with swingling, forger, burglary, murder. So far from it law and religion are glorified by the very slanders. But turn the tables and a federal court and jury will discover that society is on the precipice of anarchy."[13]

Boldfaced names from American history frequently graced the *Mercury's* pages. On May 10, 1790, Benjamin Franklin wrote in its pages to Noah Webster that he was surprised to find several new words had been introduced into "our parliamentary language." Franklin was not amused. He wrote: "For example, I find a verb formed from the substantive notice: 'I should not have noticed this, were it not,' etc . . . If you should happen to be of my opinion with respect to these innovations, you will use your authority in reprobating them. The Latin language, long they have used in distributing knowledge among the different nations of Europe, is daily more and more neglected."[14]

Thomas Paine wrote Babcock in 1805, asking him to print a letter he'd sent earlier: "My last letter (the 8th) is the most important of any I have published. I have been disappointed in not seeing it in your paper. I have reason to believe the matters therein stated will be taken up at the next meeting of Congress, and the inquiry at that time, will not be sufficiently understood by those who had not an opportunity of seeing that letter. I know the feds want to keep that letter out of sight."

The *Mercury* also published a January 1, 1795, essay, "A News-Boy's Address to the Readers of the Mercury," which included:

For this, I tript it, o'er the Town
And fpread the Mercury, up and down.[15]

The newspaper particularly opposed what Babcock thought was a growing theocracy in the new country. To one writer's suggestion that the preamble of the Constitution include a mention of the country's belief in "the one living and true God," a letter signed simply "Elihu," he responded: "A low-minded man may imagine that God, like a foolish old man, will think Himself slighted and dishonored if not complimented."[16]

In addition, the *Mercury* was home to two-fisted political satire. The newspaper published works such as "The Echo," pugnacious couplet poetry written mostly by Richard Alsop, a member of the Connecticut Wits, a group of mostly Yale graduates that included Babcock's early business partner, Joel Barlow.[17] Over pints at the downtown Black Horse Tavern, the men helped form the myth that would be America—though as a body of work, their poetry was too infused with optimism to survive subsequent ages.[18] (Maybe they would have been perfectly at home reading, or writing, the hopeful *Epic of America*.) The Wits were mostly Federalists, Calvinists, and neoclassicists for whom poetry was an "elegant avocation."[19]

The *Mercury* was not the first Babcock newspaper. Before moving to the Hartford area, Elisha published a paper in Massachusetts. The family came to Connecticut so Elisha could run a paper mill that sat at what is now near the border of East Hartford and Manchester, Conn., along the Hockanum River.[20]

At first it looked as if the family had made a huge mistake leaving their Massachusetts home. In 1778 their mill burned to the ground under suspicious circumstances, at a loss of more than five thousand pounds. Even worse, reams of paper and rags were destroyed in the fire. Mills could be rebuilt, but rags, which were used to make paper,

Hannah Bunce Watson.

were in short supply. A paper mill could not run without a rag delivery system.[21] The publisher of the *Courant*, the widow Hannah Bunce Watson, petitioned the state assembly for a lottery to raise money to rebuild the mill. The assembly approved it, the lottery was a success, the mill was rebuilt, and—rag collection system back in place—the mill came under the management of Babcock.[22] The family then moved to the capital city at the urging of Barlow, an acerbic writer who on his graduation from Yale College wrote a friend, "We are not the first men in the world to have broke loose from college without fortune to puff us into public notice, [but] if ever virtue [and merit] are to be rewarded, it is in America."[23]

Both the *Courant* and the *Mercury* surged ahead in 1792, when Congress passed the Post Office Act. The law not only transformed the postal service into what was arguably the "central administrative apparatus of an independent state," but it helped transform newspapers into something viable and influential.[24] Before the act, postal carriers were not required to deliver newspapers. Carriers were happy to deliver newspapers from one printer to the other, but home delivery was rare. Readers of newspapers mostly purchased them on the street, or they went to the newspaper offices to buy a copy.

Once people could enjoy home delivery by mail, readership exploded.[25] No one could have predicted the effect that would have on newspaper circulation, and newspapers' influence.[26] Suddenly, printers could ship newspapers for pennies, and they did. By 1830 the postal service was delivering two million more newspapers than letters.[27]

But even that boost wasn't enough to make newspapers lucrative. One historian estimates that just 5 percent of families subscribed to newspapers. So in addition to bookselling, to supplement their income Babcock and Barlow sold an almanac whose content was lifted from a similar publication by Isaac Bickerstaff, a London astrologer. With no copyright laws to dissuade them, the duo largely plagiarized Bickerstaff, and for that they were chided in the pages of their competitor, the *Courant*.

Printed admonishments between newspaper publishers were common in the early American press. In one 1817 brief, the *Courant* called a story that ran earlier that week in the *Mercury* a "base and malignant falsehood."[28] The *Mercury* gave as good as it got, but most of the carping was for show. Each newspaper tended to reprint the other's stories, and a letter to the editor in the *Courant* might just as often take to task something that had run in the *Mercury*.

Babcock continued to expand his printing empire. He printed the almanac, poetry, and hymnals, including a popular revamping of hymns from Isaac Watts. He printed work by his friend Noah Webster.[29] He sold books wholesale from New York to buyers in Louisiana, South Carolina, and the West Indies.

Babcock also participated in civic goings-on, as would any self-respecting newspaper publisher. He served on a committee to improve the town's schools. He gave speeches. He hawked his paper. Between the farm, the well, the newspapers, and the bookselling, the family thrived.

The Babcock family had six children, five of whom survived to adulthood. That was about the average family size at the time.[30] For the most part, colonial and early American (white) women believed their duty was to bear as many children as possible—preferably sons, who could help with the family business, which was often farming. Only as the new country gave birth to itself, (white) women began to push for a kind of equal footing with their menfolk that included a say in family size.[31] In early Hartford, this option was not available to most African American women, 90 percent of whom lived in slavery.[32]

The Babcocks are listed in the country's first census in 1790 as free and white. They owned no slaves, though slavery was present in the state (more on that later). When Elisha Babcock died of pneumonia at age sixty-eight on April 7, 1821, he was buried in the Old South Cemetery of Hartford's Second Congregational Church, now known as South Church. The *Mercury* continued publishing, though it is unclear who conducted the actual business. Some speculate the Babcock family—Dolly among them, until her death in 1832—kept the press rolling until the paper's demise in 1833.

The family saltbox became home for an unmarried son and daughter, Col. James and Dolly, named for her mother. James Babcock was a sales agent for a man named Ira Todd, who sold among other goods French burr millstones, considered the best stones for milling flour and grain.[33] Col. Babcock also served on a committee to raise money to aid people injured in a fire in Virginia. His business was frequently mentioned in *Courant* ads selling Sicily lemons and wax calf-skins of the highest quality, and asking for donations of long hair that would be used to stuff mattresses.[34] (Hair mattresses were considered a step up from a stack of hemlock boughs.) When Miss Dolly Babcock, the daughter, joined her parents in death in 1871, the *Courant* erroneously trumpeted that she was, at age ninety, the oldest Hartford resident to die that year. In fact, that honor fell to Mrs. Tabitha Camp, who bested Dolly Babcock's time on earth by a year and a half.[35]

An 1877 real estate notice offered—"for sale cheap"—"the property known as the Dolly Babcock homestead," situated south of the home of a professor on a lot that was roughly two hundred by three hundred feet.[36] The simple, high-pitched roofs of Hartford (the center-chimney Cape Cods and saltboxes still popular in New England) had given way to more ornate styles of architecture such as double-homes (or townhomes).[37] To enable construction of the newly styled homes to go quickly, state legislators passed a law that shingles shipped from New York no longer required inspection.[38]

In 1890 the Babcock saltbox was nearly one hundred years old and deep into a slide into disrepair. Despite its historical significance there was not much discussion about preserving it. It was, simply, an old house in a neighborhood that was making way for newer, fancier homes, including a yellow mansion that had sat at the northeast corner of the Babcock plot since the 1820s. That mansion was home to several generations of Trinity (first called Washington College) presidents and faculty members.

In 1896, with little fanfare, the Babcock house was torn down to make room for a gracious new house for the widow of a state Republican Party scion.[39] What had been the Babcock's one-hundred-acre farm was carved up for yards, and the name of Babcock was consigned to the history books—and to a street in the Frog Hollow neighborhood.

2. *An Opportunity for Each*

COLONEL POPE COMES TO TOWN AND HELPS

BUILD AN INDUSTRIAL POWERHOUSE

One cool spring day in 1878, a Boston train pulled in to Hartford's Italianate station with a spindly, top-heavy bicycle that would change manufacturing forever. The year had already seen incredible mechanical advances. A commercial telephone exchange built with carriage bolts and teapot handles had opened in New Haven.[1] Thomas Edison had applied for a patent for his cylinder phonograph after testing it by recording the nursery rhyme "Mary Had a Little Lamb."[2] John Philip Holland had launched a submarine in New Jersey.[3] Modernity was being birthed down a canal of wires and plugs. It was simply looking for the proper delivery room.

In 1850 Hartford's population was 13,555. By 1870 the population had more than doubled to nearly 38,000; by 1890, to 53,230. The town by 1900 boasted nearly 80,000 residents—an increase of six times over—and the town's boundary bulged west.

What had happened? Industry. Manufacturing came to Frog Hollow, and with it, innovators, planners, immigrants, and farmers anxious to step away from their plows and work at a job where their fortunes were not ruled by the weather.[4]

Starting in the 1850s and for a little over a half century, Frog Hol-

Colonel Albert Pope.

Hartford's Population, 1850–1900

YEAR	POPULATION OF HARTFORD
1850	13,555
1860	29,152
1870	37,743
1880	42,551
1890	53,230
1900	79,850

low was the center of a stunning array of factories that helped give birth to a modern age. Bicycles were manufactured there. Sewing machines. Tools. Cars. People moved from near and far to live in Perfect Sixes that were built within walking distance of factories where jobs were plentiful. The city laid trolley tracks and then added more and more tracks to accommodate the boom.

Starting with a colonial grist mill, like begat like.

The man accompanying that bike on the train, Albert Pope, was a restless Civil War veteran and an industrialist who was as skilled at promoting innovation as he was at manufacturing it. He was bringing his baby to Hartford because that's where the innovators of the day were changing manufacturing forever.

When Pope's train stopped in Hartford, he hopped onto his fifty-six-inch Duplex Excelsior, a relatively unsafe mechanism with a large front wheel, a small back one, and a penchant for pitching riders over the handlebars. Pope asked for directions and then headed off for the Weed Sewing Machine Company a mile away.[5] What better way to convince a manufacturer to take on a new product, Pope thought, than to demonstrate that product in person?

A bike was an unusual sight in Hartford streets, and on his ride Pope attracted the attention of laughing, wide-eyed children, who fell in behind him. By the time he arrived at the brick factory on Capitol Avenue, he was followed by scores of children—and a few energetic adults eager for excitement.

Pope was pedaling to see George A. Fairfield, a talented machinist who met him at the Weed factory door and rather quickly caught Pope's enthusiasm for the bike's potential. Fairfield's employees had been churning out sewing machines. With a few modifications, Fairfield believed they could use similar methods for drop-forging bicycle hubs and steering wheels.[6]

This was one of many partnerships that turned the Connecticut

1898 Pope Columbia "Standard of the World" ad.

River Valley, writes Bruce D. Epperson in *Peddling Bicycles to America: The Rise of an Industry*, into the nineteenth century's version of Silicon Valley. The best and brightest minds were drawn to opportunities for cash and creativity in the lower Connecticut Valley—most specifically Hartford, and in particular, Frog Hollow.[7]

If Frog Hollow was Silicon Valley, then George Fairfield was Steve Wozniak. Fairfield wasn't as concerned with the finished product as he was with the production process. To Fairfield, every article produced in Frog Hollow was a manufacturing puzzle to be solved, and the factories that lined Capitol Avenue created a complex and robust economy with ample opportunity for problem-solving. In addition to Sharps rifles, Frog Hollow factories turned out Weed sewing machines and, eventually, Pope's bicycles and electric- and gas-powered automobiles, as well as a wide array of tools.

With the help of Christopher M. Spencer, an inventor, the Weed company (and later the Hartford Machine Screw Co.) set the standard for efficiency and innovation. For a while, Weed's factory was larger than the better-known Colt's Armory.[8] For a few years, announcements about the latest technology ran in the *Courant* nearly daily in a regular column, "Manufacturing Notes." On just one day in 1878, the column announced that Weed was developing a "twin needle" sewing machine for use in shoe and harness work. Down the street, the workers at Billings & Spencer were perfecting a device that could be used for clipping horses—or shearing sheep. The device allowed the clipper to finish clipping a horse in an hour or less.[9] How long it took to clip a horse without benefit of Billings & Spencer's new device is lost history, but if the breathless *Courant* column is any indication, an hour was a big deal.

For Pope, the bicycle was only his latest obsession. While visiting the 1876 Philadelphia Centennial Exposition, Pope saw a two-wheeled velocipede with an enormous front wheel and a smaller, solid rubber tire in the back. The contraption had been around for

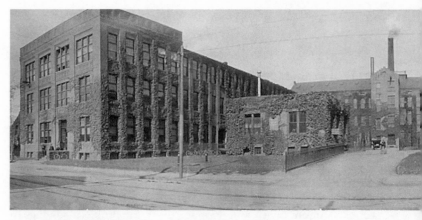

"Pope Manufacturing Co." Haines Photo Co. Copyright Claimant.
Pope Mfg. Co. #2, Hartford, Conn. c. 1909. Retrieved from Library of
Congress, www.loc.gov/item/2007662033

centuries, but the 1870s public disdained it. Horses were frightened
by it, and municipal ordinances banned it from parks and avenues.

None of that deterred Pope. He was ready for a new venture, and
within a year of witnessing the velocipede, he had sunk $3,000 (about
$125,000 in today's money) into the manufacturing of bicycles.[10]

Fairfield was sold on Pope's contraption, but Weed's board of directors did not share his excitement. Fortunately, Fairfield saw the big
picture—and the future. For generations, work in Frog Hollow had
consisted of labor-intensive efforts performed with the help of draft
animals. Yet water that turned millstones became steam power, steam
became combustion engines, and engines became electricity. New
employees were trading rakes and shovels for machines that would
deliver the country into a new industrial age.[11] With industrialization,
work shifted to capital and animals were retired in favor of machines,
which seemed bound by no limits.[12] Obsolete draft animals were
replaced by horses, which would soon be replaced by mechanisms

powered by steam. Fairfield knew that if Weed could capture even a piece of the coming market, the company's shareholders would walk away wealthy. That was part of his argument to his board, and the directors rather reluctantly voted to accept an order to manufacture fifty bicycles as prototypes.

At first it seemed the directors' reticence was the proper response. Weed workers encountered one difficulty after another learning to forge the bicycle frame, shape the wheel rims, and fabricate steel handlebars and cranks. Fairfield was adamant, though, that this would be Weed's next success, and after much trial and error the workers turned out a bicycle that weighed sixty pounds. It was christened the Columbia, the first commercial self-propelled vehicle in America. ("Columbia" became a generic name for the bicycle, as "Kodak" later was for the camera.)

In Frog Hollow machinists anxious to try out the latest theories of production teamed with businessmen such as Pope to take advantage of Hartford's astonishing machine tool companies, which would include Pratt & Whitney Machine Tool (that later became the behemoth aircraft manufacturer) and Billings & Spencer.

Pope was a restless man who had moved from manufacturing shoes to building wildly popular cigarette-rolling machines that fit into a coat pocket and eliminated finger stains. Pope also briefly manufactured an air pistol that sold for three dollars and was, according to an 1876 *Forest and Stream* advertisement, "recommended by Gen. W. T. Sherman," the controversial military strategist known for his "total war" approach to the enemy.

By the mid-1850s, Frog Hollow's colonial families with names such as Babcock, Russ, and Hungerford had sold their farms. Every few weeks, more excavation chewed up Frog Hollow farmland. At one point a new building planned near the Weed Sewing Machine plant was delayed because there simply weren't enough bricks.[13] Over time, trolley tracks were laid down newly drawn streets. The neighborhood was a hive of activity. Despite the poverty of some of its residents— many of them immigrants—the town was about to boast the highest per capita income in the United States.[14]

The impact of this shift cannot be overstated. While machinists harnessed new technology, the middle class "emerged as a moral and political power."[15] Manufacturers and industrialists already engaged in innovation in Vermont and Massachusetts looked south and saw Frog Hollow's farmland, fed by abundant water power along with the city's recently laid tracks; they moved swiftly to buy land, build factories, and hire workers. The boom time started with the 1850s opening of the Sharps Rifle factory in the area where once a gristmill had stood.[16]

In 1820 William H. Imlay, a shopkeeper, bought a flaxseed oil mill at the western end of what is now Hartford's Capitol Avenue but was then a dirt road known as Oil Mill Lane. The area around the mill became known as Imlay's Upper Mills.[17] Mills were so important that early American towns were often laid out around them. During King Philip's War in the 1670s, the mill in Springfield, Mass., was destroyed and some residents left for towns that still had working mills.[18] Without a mill, settlers spent hours with a pestle and mortar—an average of two hours a day, in fact—just to prepare corn for a family's daily bread.

Mill owners were so prized that they were sometimes given free land for their business.[19] Because their mills were so important, mill owners were generally considered town leaders. Imlay was a part of a group of Hartford residents whose members in 1827 were appointed to study the feasibility of erecting a fireproof building where town records could be stored. Up to then, the town clerk—usually a man who held the office for life—kept the records in his home or office.[20]

Like the machinists and toolmakers after him, Imlay was industrious to the extreme. One day, evidently without a thought to the history of the place, Imlay removed the last bit of an old riverside Dutch fort in Hartford, the site where Europeans first made a mark on the land.[21] Imlay wanted to dam a marsh, perhaps to increase his water power.

The Sharps Rifle factory opened near the mill, where water could run the early machinery. The name of the street now known as Capitol Avenue frequently changed to reflect local industries. Oil Mill Lane was later known as Rifle Lane.[22] For a time, when Trinity College anchored one end, the street was known as College. It was also known—at least a portion of it—as Stowe Street, for the famous author Harriet Beecher Stowe, who lived in a more affluent part of town known as Nook Farm, just north of Frog Hollow.[23]

Sharps came to the hollow at the request of George H. Penfield, who owned land in the neighborhood and was a Sharps shareholder. Penfield believed in the abundant resources of Frog Hollow, and for a while, a street in the neighborhood was named after him, though it was eventually changed to Putnam.[24]

Patented in 1848, Christian Sharps's breech-loading rifle quickly replaced the cumbersome muzzleloader.[25] For Frog Hollow, the Sharps factory was a goose laying one golden egg after another. During the Civil War, the Sharps rifle was popular with both U.S.

and Confederate troops.[26] The Sharps company was paid a royalty of one dollar per rifle, or nearly thirty in today's dollars. Henry Ward Beecher, who was the younger brother of Harriet, said that one Sharps—later known as "Old Reliable"—carried more moral weight than one hundred Bibles, a statement that confounded some of the members of his Brooklyn, N.Y., church. Newspapers carried stories that rifles were shipped in boxes labeled "books" and "Bibles" to aid people in Kansas who opposed slavery. The press had a field day with "Beecher's Bibles."[27] Throughout the war, the *Daily Courant* carried notices that the factory was hiring.[28] Unemployment was minimal.

Sharps was the first factory of any significant size in Frog Hollow, but it was quickly followed by others. Jobs brought people like Charles Billings, a machinist of old New England stock. One of Billings's ancestors, Richard, had been granted six acres in Hartford in 1640, but later the family moved north to Vermont. At age seventeen Billings began an apprenticeship with Robbins & Lawrence Co., gun makers and machinists in Windsor, Vermont. As was common at the time, Billings's family agreed to provide board, lodging, and clothing in exchange for his instruction and a salary of fifty, then fifty-five, then sixty cents for the first, second, and third year of labor. Billings served his indenture then moved to Hartford to work at Colt's Patent Fire Arms Manufacturing Co., which was then considered the premier gun maker on the East Coast.

Colt's, which was located east of the neighborhood near the Connecticut River, was also an early laboratory for many early industrial innovators. There on the oil-soaked floors, Billings worked as a die-sinker in the drop-forging department, where the machinery was complicated and expensive to maintain. Drop forge is a process used to shape metal into complex shapes by dropping a heavy hammer with a die on its face onto a piece of metal. The process involved "a rough-forming stroke in a drop forge, a pressing operation to trim off the unwanted 'flash,' and a finishing stroke in another drop forge."[29]

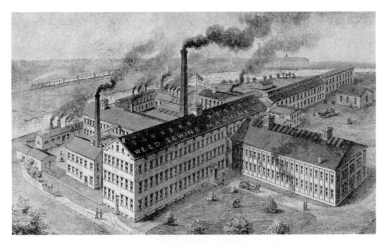

Weed Sewing Machine plant, c. 1889, Hartford, Connecticut.

In 1862 Billings moved to E. Remington & Sons in Utica, N.Y., where he began streamlining the drop-forging process and increased the company's efficiency by "40-fold," according to the 1901 *Commemorative Biographical Record of Hartford County, Conn.*[30] After saving Remington some fifty thousand dollars, he returned to Hartford in 1865 to work at Weed Sewing Machine Co., where he revolutionized drop-forging in the manufacture of the sewing machine's shuttles, the part of the machine beneath the needle that creates a lockstitch.

The reputation of Weed's machines quickly reached almost mythical proportions. "If you desire a real 'peace commissioner' in the parlor," said one *New York Times* article, "or a gold mine 'constantly on hand,' or a mint ready for 'home use' which will only require the touch of gentle hands to produce a currency the range of which is universal," then you were urged to buy a Weed sewing machine.[31]

Originally, Weed machines were made by contractors spread around the state. In the summer of 1865, sensing there was efficiency to be had in consolidation, the owners of Pratt & Whitney began building their new machine shops along Flower Street, using H. &

S. Bissell as contractor. The main building was four stories high and 150 feet long, and Weed was one of the early tenants.[32]

The next year, 1866, Weed took over the space formerly filled by Sharps, which was eventually purchased by showman P. T. Barnum, who moved that operation to Bridgeport. Weed officials eventually bought the entire factory, and many Sharps employees stayed on to make sewing machines.[33] In the manufacturing process there was not much difference between guns and sewing machines.[34]

The sewing machines sold for a princely sixty to two hundred dollars, depending on the cabinetry. Some of the fancier cases were made of black walnut and were decorated with inlaid pearl. The popularity of the machines is hard to square with the economics of the time. The Civil War was followed by a six-and-a-half-year financial crisis in the United States, and household income hovered around ten dollars a week. A sewing machine was a substantial investment, but consumers ordered the machines anyway and sometimes waited months for delivery.[35]

That same year, Weed bought the most ornate horse carriage imaginable (from George S. Evarts on Albany Ave.) for advertising and delivery purposes. The carriage alone—never mind the machines it carried—merited a three-inch write-up in the *Courant*.[36]

Owner T. E. Weed had moved operations to Hartford, but it was Billings who brought the machine to the level where it rivaled the better-known Singer machine. A *Chicago Republican* writer, in the flowery language of the day, wrote that the Hartford factory "provided with the most ingenious mechanical devices of modern invention for perfecting every part of the machine."[37] No other machine, raved one *New York Times* article, had grown so rapidly in popularity: "It would seem that this machine will soon have, and deservedly so, a world-wide reputation."[38]

At their Frog Hollow factory, workers turned out two hundred machines a day—a short five years after receiving a patent.[39] Industrial historians have given far more attention to the manufacturing of cars in American production, but sewing machines gave birth to the principles of interchangeability, which could be applied to clocks and guns and automobiles and munitions—just about anything that could be made in a factory.

Where the sewing machine actually started is unclear. Elias Howe Jr., who was born in Massachusetts, patented what's considered the world's first sewing machine in 1846, though there were machines that accomplished the same task before his. Howe gave credit to his wife, Elizabeth J. Ames Howe, who, he told others, created in two hours what he had struggled to finish for fourteen years. Whatever his wife's contribution, Howe applied for a patent in his own name, according to Russell Conwell, a minister and orator who served with Howe in the Civil War. In a speech Conwell would give more than five thousand times, called "Acres of Diamonds," he said Howe's "wife made up her mind one day they would starve to death if there wasn't something or other invented pretty soon, and so in two hours she invented the sewing-machine. Of course he took out the patent in his name. Men always do that."[40] Prior to Elizabeth Howe's breakthrough, Howe earned nine dollars a week as a machinist, and Elizabeth, with their three children, sometimes took in sewing to help with family finances.

As with most new technology, early adopters anxious to protect their investments hired good lawyers, and sometimes history remembers the ones who were successful not so much in the lab but in court. (Edison brought skills to the public sphere both as an inventor and as a scrappy battler in court.) Howe spent five years in court suing Isaac Singer for patent infringement in what the newspapers of the day called the Sewing Machine Wars. Howe eventually won.[41]

There was at the time no equal to the rapid adoption of the sewing machine by the American public. Between Howe's 1854 court victory and 1870, some 1.5 million machines were built.[42] Of those, 70,000 came from the Weed company in Hartford. In 1869 Weed produced 20,000 machines, and nearly 30,000 the year after that.[43] The Weed Sewing Machine Co. completed its one hundred thousandth machine in September 1871. The machine's relative high cost did not stop its fans. One account of a Weed tour in the *Courant* called the machines "a kind of iron poetry." The brief was signed "Old Curiosity."[44]

The factory proper was one of the largest in the city, and the machine was a marvel in "take-up," or the process by which the needle looped around the thread beneath the fabric being sewed. For that, consumers could thank the man Pope was so anxious to hire, George A. Fairfield, designer and patent holder of the two-lever system that allowed this smooth dance between needle and thread:

> As the needle bar passes down and the point of the needle enters the goods, this "take up" remains stationary until the needle has penetrated to the eye, when it passes down rapidly until the needle has reached its lowest descent, throwing out the slack to form a loop for the shuttle to pass through, and is again stationary until the shuttle passes the loop and the needle bar commences to rise, when it ascends rapidly until the loop is taken up, when it is again stationary while the needle bar goes up to tighten the stitch, the "take up" in the meantime holding the thread firmly until the feed has given the desired length of stitch.[45]

Genius.

The machine won honors at fairs in Pennsylvania, Chicago, and New Hampshire, as well as the behemoth Windham County Fair in Brooklyn, Conn. The machine also won international acclaim, including three awards in 1873 and a "best family sewing machine" award at an exposition in Paris.[46] This was exciting news back home, considering the company had sent two of its three models strictly for exhibition, and not for competition. "There is no boast, therefore, in claiming this award . . . places the Company's beyond the reach of rivalry," said a subsequent advertisement's humble-brag.[47] One testimonial from circa 1874 listed the ways in which the Weed machine was superior, including, from a female customer, "Because it never vexes me."[48]

With Weed and others, Frog Hollow's factory district grew, and by 1880 the neighborhood's streets were laid out and the manufacturing heart of the city was beating fast. The increasingly crowded neighborhood drew tradesmen like Charles Thurston, a machinist who lived with his family at 18 Putnam Street. Thurston was one of nine hundred men who lost their tools in a suspicious fire at Colt's in 1864. The fire was detected around 8 a.m. in the morning of February 4. The Portland brownstone walls and slate roof—thought to be fireproof at the time—were destroyed. The factory's yellow pine floors had been soaked for nearly a decade with machinery oil, and when ignited they went up like a match—"faster than a man could run," according to one eyewitness. Neighbors gathered and watched from nearby buildings as the ornate Byzantine dome fell within an hour of the fire's detection.[49] The *Courant* speculated that the blaze, which destroyed the older part of the factory, home to the most expensive machinery, was the work of an arsonist, though the miscreant was never found.[50] Though he had to replace his tools, the booming economy delivered Thurston work fairly quickly and in his own neighborhood.

While Thurston was losing his tools, his neighbor, Peter Kenney, was trying to extinguish the flames. Kenney, also a Frog Hollow resident, Irish immigrant, and Colt's employee, had been a volunteer firefighter for three years before the fire. He and others tried to save the factory, but the water supply was inadequate. The fire was especially damaging because it was during the height of the factory's Civil War production. From the *New York Times*: "Those who had friends employed at the armory were foremost in the rush, and wives, mothers, and sisters, with anxious looks, made eager haste to the meadows. We have never witnessed so much excitement on a similar occasion. Seventeen or eighteen hundred workmen aroused by the sudden cry of fire in their midst could not well maintain among them all, perfect composure; and thus it was that in some instances the widest excitement ensued."

The fire was considered the worst calamity to hit Hartford up to that time, and there was concern that Colt's would not recover; but the company did recover and the fire hastened the formation of a paid town fire department. For Kenney, the firefighter, the Colt's disaster was the start of a big year. He continued to fight fires from the No. 6 firehouse downtown. On Christmas evening that year, he married his childhood sweetheart from Ireland, downtown at St. Patrick's Church. They celebrated their fiftieth wedding anniversary there in 1914.

The fire also gave rise to the insurance industry, which would carry Hartford's economy for generations. After the Colt's fire, Elizabeth Colt, widow of company founder Samuel, decided to rebuild, and the new five-story factory opened just three years later.[51] The following year, Mark Twain toured the facilities and became an immediate fan. He wrote:

> On every floor is a dense wilderness of strange iron machines . . . a tangled forest of rods, bars, pulleys, wheels, and all the imaginable and unimaginable forms of mechanism. There are machines to cut all the various parts of a pistol, roughly, from the original steel: machines to trim them down and polish them: machines to brand and number them: machines to bore the barrels out: machines to rifle them: machines that shave them down neatly to a proper size, as deftly as one would shave a candle in a lathe.[52]

Twain was so impressed with Hartford and its industry (and the presence of his American publisher there) that he moved his family to the city in 1874, and nearly spent his way into the poorhouse building a sprawling brick mansion in the Nook Farm neighborhood. There he would write some of his best-known work, including *The Adventures of Tom Sawyer* and *The Adventures of Huckleberry Finn*.

"I think this is the best built and handsomest town I have ever seen," he wrote.[53] Albert Pope thought so, too. But for every boom there is a bust. In a four-year period that ended in 1876, Weed production dropped by half. Given the businesses that had already left the city or had much reduced their production, people were nervous. Pope bought the Weed company so he could have his own factory. The *Courant* sought to reassure a nervous city, and called Pope's purchase "one of the most important business transactions that has taken place in Hartford for a long time, but it contains no implication whatever of any removal from here. The only change is one of ownership."[54] The manufacturing of sewing machines continued alongside that of bicycles for another ten years, until Pope phased out sewing machines to focus exclusively on bikes and, eventually, automobiles.

With Hartford as a magnet for laborers looking for good jobs, the *Courant* reported that farms around the state were being abandoned in droves. Members gathered for a Dairymen's meeting in Hartford in 1892 and decided to compile a list of abandoned farms, and old mills. "The time is remembered by many when almost every waterfall on the thousands of streams which drain the hills and water the valleys of New England turned a wheel," said one report.[55] By 1910 all new industrial development in Frog Hollow was basically complete. In a heady fifty-some years, the city had gone from farmland to industrial giant.

In 1912 the *Courant* carried a story that extolled the city's embrace of manufacturing with the headline, "When It's Made in Hartford, It's Made Right":

But one reason—aside from that of civic pride and the activity of her citizens—can be ascribed to the advance Hartford has made, and that reason is the manner in which the city has kept up with the times. Old manufacturing methods have given way to the most modern kind in this city just as soon as new methods were invented; in many cases they found their birthplace in this city. For instance, when the field for manufacturing bicycles proved better than the field for sewing-machines, a local company manufacturing sewing machines immediately took up the work of making bicycles.[56]

Because the various manufacturers weren't competing with one another, newcomers were able to rely on already-established businesses for a leg up. Settled into its new four-story-high factory on Capitol Avenue, Hartford Machine (now Stanadyne, based in Windsor, Conn.) began to develop what became an automatic high-speed lathe. The new company originally began in a spare room in the Weed factory.[57] The Frog Hollow incubator system continued, and companies were able to rely on each other for improvement in their disparate products.

Pope manufacturers knew the early design of the bicycle was faulty. The frame was sturdy but unless riders rode with their weight thrown toward the back, they would be pitched over the front wheel. Brave early consumers were forced to figure that out for themselves. Twain himself elected to take lessons, after which he wrote an unpublished manuscript titled "Taming the Bicycle." A boater all his life (his pen name, after all, came from riverboats), he insisted on calling the handlebar a tiller and ended the essay with, "Get a bicycle. You will not regret it, if you live."[58]

Other manufacturing companies such as Ford and Singer built stores to sell their products. Pope did not. If a consumer wanted to purchase a bike, the buyer had to go to a hardware store or visit an agent who sold Columbias.[59] That quirk did not seem to keep customers away, and Pope knew it wouldn't. A Columbia was a specialty

Early bicycles were mostly ridden by men. Female cyclists had to first be convinced to wear bloomers (or "rational dress") to allow for peddling. 1895. Courtesy of Library of Congress Prints and Photographs Division, Washington, D.C. 20540.

item, and so was its owner. Pope was appealing to the modern man—most riders were male—who was willing to stand out in a crowd and spend no small amount of energy tracking down his product. Other manufacturing luminaries, including Henry Ford, came to visit the Hartford plant for inspiration. Before Ford became famous for it, Pope's employees used interchangeable bicycle wheels, tires, and gear-shaft drive mechanisms, a technique they learned from Fairfield and one borrowed by Ford with great success.

By 1896 the plant had a thousand machines turning out screws at tens of thousands per minute, according to a 1918 *American Machinist* magazine article. The machines included "milling machines, turret lathes, screw machines, grinding machines, drilling and boring machines."[60] Within ten years, Pope stood before a crowd in Philadelphia and said that American-made bicycles had taken over the world market—in part because the Hartford factory included an entire

Early (and bizarre)
Columbia bicycle ad.

division devoted to modifying the product to suit the riders of a particular country's needs.[61] Pope's Hartford operations grew to include
five factories that employed four thousand people.[62] Meanwhile, in
an 1896 interview with the London-based publication *Cycling World*,
Pope said there was no limit to the bicycle market. At $125 the bicycle
was pricey for the average consumer, yet sales quickly hit one thousand a year. George Keller, who designed Pope's factory housing,
told his wife that Pope couldn't even sell *him* a bicycle because the
factory had orders they couldn't begin to fulfill. (Keller also designed
Bushnell Park's "Soldiers and Sailors Memorial Arch," of Portland
brownstone.[63] His ashes are buried in the arch along with the ashes
of his wife, Mary.)

While the bicycle design was vamped and revamped, the Hartford plant was among the first in the country to switch from coal to
kerosene fuel.[64] Ever the competitor, Pope began buying patents as

quickly as he could. Ford did the same thing. Pope also employed a knack for self-promotion unrivaled by any of his contemporaries, save perhaps Barnum. In this, Ford could not compete. Pope once told an interviewer that his perfect employee was the most faithful fellow in the world. "He has been in my employ for 17 years, yet he has never even asked for a holiday. He works both day and night, is never asleep or intoxicated, and though I pay him more than $250,000 a year, I consider that he costs me nothing. His name is Advertisement."[65]

Pope mostly treated his (human) employees as would a benevolent dictator. He was generous at Christmas, and before there was such a thing as workers' insurance, he was quick to send money to the families of ill employees. An 1893 magazine article praised Pope for his factory's washrooms, which included hot *and* cold water sinks, as well as a library and reading room and a stable for workers to store their bicycles, since most of them rode to work.[66]

That benevolence shifted a bit when workers threatened to join a machinists' union in 1901. The factory shut down briefly but opened again when negotiators agreed to let workers form committees, though not a union.[67] Pope also agreed to a nine-hour day and a raise in pay.

Many of Frog Hollow's industrialists had served their apprenticeships beneath the blue dome of Colt's in the southeastern part of the city, but not Pope. Yet both Pope and Colt understood that their fortunes depended on their workers' happiness. Pope purchased land that had been the old Bartholomew family farm to the southwest of his factory, and donated ninety acres for the creation of a park. Designed by the famous Olmsted brothers, the park included tennis courts and a rolling lawn. Pope said, "I believe that a large part of the success of any manufacturing enterprise depends on the health, happiness and orderly life of its employees."[68]

To hawk his bikes, Pope sponsored races and a bicycle-riding school and promoted public parks as tremendous places to test a bike.

He countered certain clergy members' assertions that bike riding on Sunday was wrong with the suggestion that churches build bike barns similar to the ones outside his factory, so worshippers could ride to church. And wasn't exercise a form of worshipping God?

He also founded the League of American Wheelmen, pushed for better roads through a magazine devoted to the joys of cycling, and endowed positions in highway engineering at the Massachusetts Institute of Technology to make the roads smoother.[69] Without good roads, Pope knew, bicycles were little more than expensive paperweights.

But as with the Weed bust of a few years earlier, the bicycle boom was relatively short-lived. By the turn of the last century, consumers began to crave transportation that did not require pedaling. Pope's company was slightly slow to catch on, and for a few months they suffered from overproduction amid falling demand. But then Pope started a Motor Carriage Department. And there Pope applied the same energy to the creation of his version of the horseless carriage. The first product was an electric car, the "Mark III," in 1897. Using technology honed in the manufacture of bicycles, the Pope plant "was truly the nursery of the infant [automobile] industry," according to one observer.[70] Just as they had figured out how to keep bicycle riders from pitching over the handlebars, Pope engineers began to finesse electric motors.

In short order, American consumers could choose from the Pope-Tribune, the Pope-Waverly, the Pope-Toledo, and the Pope-Hartford, a midpriced auto that went for $3,200 and was priced squarely between Ford models that sold for $1,000–$2,000 and the higher-priced Packard at $7,000.[71] By 1899 Pope had all but single-handedly turned Hartford into the center of the automotive world.[72]

Two of Pope's employees, George H. Day and Hiram Percy Maxim, set out to create workable engines, but Day's heart was not in gasoline-powered contraptions. In fact, by one account, when faced with an engine, he shook his head and asked if the engines had to have so many gears and so much oil. "We are on the wrong track," Day was supposed to have said. "No one will buy a carriage that has to have all that greasy machinery in it. It might be that young fellows like you . . . would buy a few of them as interesting toys, but that would be only a drop in the bucket."[73]

Pope wholeheartedly agreed, "because you can't get people to sit over an explosion."[74] (Sigh.)

While Pope's employees focused on perfecting a two-seated electric car—also called the Columbia—Midwest manufacturers, Henry Ford among them, were aiming for the middle market with mass-produced (and cheaper) manufacturing. In 1899 Pope's company produced more than half of the cars in the United States.[75] The *Courant* predicted in 1905 that the Columbia car was showing massive improvement, due in part to the addition of nickel-steel parts. The company would continue its production of electric delivery wagons and trucks and was entertaining large advance orders.[76]

But along with Thomas Edison, Ford was as talented as an industrialist as he was skilled at lawyering up. Pope and Ford rather quickly went to court, and eventually Pope's legal issues with Ford took too much time and energy. That, along with his reluctance to pursue a workable gas engine, relegated Albert Pope to the edges of history. People in Hartford know him. People in Frog Hollow certainly know him. But the world at large knows Henry Ford and his vision of assembly line manufacturing—something he borrowed from his Hartford competitor. History is not always fair.

In other Frog Hollow factories a combination of bad luck and bad planning made the machines go dark, which eventually left the neighborhood without a manufacturing base. In June 1875 the *Courant* carried a story about rumors that Sharps Rifle would move to Bridgeport. It was evident, said the story, that the gun was "the best breech-loading arm manufactured in the world," and the article called for Hartford capitalists to fight to keep Sharps, as "we have not so many manufactories here that we can afford to spare any of them."[77]

In 1886 the Weed company announced at its annual stockholder meeting that the capital stock of the company had shrunk from $600,000 to $240,000.[78] From a high of seventy-five dollars a share, Weed shares had slipped to five dollars.

In July 1914 Billings & Spencer paid $250,000 for the old Columbia motorcar plant on Laurel Street. Columbia's time had passed, while Billings & Spencer had just added two hundred workers to their workforce of six hundred. The company intended to expand its production of wrenches and small tools. The purchase included 8¼ acres of land, roughly 2¼ of which were buildings. The company made twenty-three different kinds of wrenches and with its drop-forge work had a direct line to Detroit and its car factories. The factory was near the railroad, and rents in the neighborhood were "reasonable," according to the *Courant*.[79]

Despite the relative economic success of the neighborhood, Frog Hollow's business fronts didn't have the shiny windows and fancy entrances of downtown Hartford. For all the development of the previous fifty years, at the turn of the last century the place had the feel of a throwback to early Hartford. It was almost as if buildings had been put up so quickly to accommodate the influx that no one had thought of aesthetics. Not to fear. A writer in the *Courant* suggested that the prosperity of the neighborhood would eventually force establishments to catch up to the rest of the modern city.[80] The market, and consumers, would demand it.

And then the United States entered World War I, and as had happened during the Civil War, Hartford's workforce worked overtime. Between 1917 and 1918, the bulk of the state's industry was involved in defense contracting, with Hartford at the center of the effort.[81] In Frog Hollow and elsewhere, the factories that had remained essen-

Billings & Spencer plant, Laurel Street. Publisher, Chapin News Company, Hartford. Richard L. Mahoney Collection, Hartford History Center, Hartford Public Library

tially never closed during wartime, and the need for workers was unending.

Defense jobs opened the doors to a new group of workers looking for better wages. In 1916 there were 25,063 factory workers in Hartford and about 20 percent of them were women.[82] Women were considered neater than their male colleagues at Pratt, where many of them worked making drawings of the various weapons, such as Russian rifles and British guns.[83]

A 1919 *Courant* headline called the increased productivity "War's Miracles in City's Factories." The factory's armies, said the article by David D. Bidwell, swelled by fourteen thousand hands. The output of taxable goods increased by 250 percent, and at the time of the armistice in 1918, Hartford's payroll topped out at one million dollars a week, a record high.

"They drew to their home city, as a magnet draws steel filings, workmen and women from all over southern New England and in fact from many towns hundreds of miles distant," the *Courant* said. "They made their city known as one of the liveliest of live centers on the munitions map."[84] The city's cost of living increased 54 percent, but wages had grown by 80 percent. The factories began to expand their walls and hours, and more employers reverted to the Albert Pope/Samuel Colt way of doing things by offering after-work activities and events. Popular baseball teams grew into an obsession with factory leagues competing through the week.

If the war brought work for the factories, residents of Frog Hollow found themselves cutting back. A coal shortage, and an attendant rise in prices, meant that fuel was too expensive for most families. Frog Hollow residents had long been accustomed to cold furnaces, at least until November 1, the traditional date for beginning to heat homes for the winter, but in 1917 a mid-October snow tested that resolve, as "New England weather is very indifferent to the alleged shortage of fuel," according to a *Courant* article.[85] The shortage was reported at fifty million tons, and first priority was given to the defense industry. Though there were some instances of gouging and hoarding coal, most residents heeded a November 1917 *Courant* headline, "Every Coal User Must Co-operate."[86]

After World War I, Hartford wasn't precisely a sleepy town, but it had the feel of most other midsized New England cities. Downtowns were robust, though after the stores closed, all but the streetlights went dark. The latter part of the era was spent in the Depression, and though New England struggled, the northern economy remained healthier than in other parts of the country. Smaller farmers in New England, in particular, did not suffer on the same scale as their midwestern colleagues.[87] The Park (Hog) River flooded frequently, and city planners decided that miles of sandbags were not enough. In 1940 the Army Corps of Engineers began burying the river, which had come to serve as an aboveground conduit for industrial waste.

The project included nine miles of pipe, and Frog Hollow shuddered in preparation for another shift in fortunes.

After every war since the civil one, defense plants had moved to peacetime products, only to rev up again with munitions for the next war. During World War II, once again the city shifted back. This was not necessarily as seamless as adjusting a wrench or recalibrating a machine. In factories, shifting production of items between war- and peacetime could take a month or a year.[88] But when the Japanese bombed Pearl Harbor, Hartford was just two turns of a screw from being a war machine. Already the capital city had in place an infrastructure that would contribute greatly to the war effort, in both human and material capital. Already Connecticut was an industry center for aircraft manufacturing, employing 13.5 percent of the workers nationally in the field.[89]

In fact, even before the country declared war, Hartford was operating as if the country was at war already. In September 1941—three months before the attack at Pearl Harbor—the city boasted fifty-two defense-related industries.[90] On the day that will live in infamy, the *New York Times* reported that Hartford was "having growing pains. Defense work is the reason. Factories once used to turn out things like typewriters, percolators and toasters are now manufacturing war materials. Defense workers have flooded into the Nutmeg State's sedate old capital on the muddy Connecticut River."[91] By the time the war ended, Connecticut manufacturers had fulfilled more than eight billion dollars in contracts.[92]

But with peacetime the suburbs were calling, and those Frog Hollow residents who could do so began to move away from the center of the city. Ironically, the budding insurance industry would step in and make Hartford, for a while, the Insurance Capital of the World.

The idea of insuring one's self or property started in Philadelphia as an antidote to fires that periodically swept through the closely built wood structures of that town. Word spread in Hartford that James

G. Batterson, the son of a stonecutter and owner of a granite works, was preparing to offer insurance to travelers on railroads, a notoriously dangerous form of passage. One day in 1864, when Batterson ran into James Bolter, a banker, at the Hartford post office, Bolter jokingly asked him how much it would cost to insure him on his walk home to Asylum Hill (a distance of about four blocks). Batterson said, perhaps facetiously, "Two cents," which Bolter paid, and thus was born the nation's first accident policy. (Bolter was supposed to have made it home safely.)[93]

Insurance would change the face of industry as well. Frank W. Cheney of the Cheney Brothers silk manufacturing company bought the first major accident policy in May 1864.[94] A 1909 book extolled the work of the hypothetical "Mr. Engineer" and said that "wood-working machines, with the saws and knives revolving thousands of times a minute, seek in vain to mangle the hands and fingers of the workman, while cunningly devised guards permit the workman's hands to push the work along or to glide harmlessly over knives or cutters; at the same time, there being no interference with the speed or limitation of the output." All hail "safety elevators, emergency brakes, rail joints, automatic gate crossings and signals, life buoys and collapsible lifeboats, safety hatches, life guns, safety clothes lines; and methods for safeguarding the milk and food supply."[95] For a while the offices of Travelers Insurance included what they called a "Chamber of Industrial Horrors" for visitors to study photographs of explosions, open elevator shafts, and machinery before protective devices had been installed. Defective chains, broken cogs, snapped tubes and rivets—it was all on display.[96]

For all the exhibit's trumpeting of a safer work environment, workers were still routinely injured and sent home to Frog Hollow to exist on the kindness of neighbors or local churches. By some estimates, industrial accidents occurred two million times a year, and that number was far and away higher than any other statistic in any part of the world, according to a 1911 *Courant* article.[97] In 1910 the Aetna Life Insurance Company published *Safeguards for the Prevention of Industrial Accidents*, because according to that book's first chapter, "The toll of human life and limb being exacted by modern industry has reached such startling proportions as to be a serious menace to our national welfare."[98]

This was evident both in the number of deaths and dismemberments, and in the laws that were being passed to prevent such events. The machinery heated up, and in February 1912 E. Sidney Berry, counsel of the Hartford Steam Boiler Inspection & Insurance Company, spoke to a gathering of insurance agents: "This is a great country for liberty, but we lay more emphasis on liberty of property than we do on liberty of life."[99] Owners had not taken proper steps because, according to Berry, accidents didn't cost them enough. After all, when railroads found it expensive to pay recompense to injured passengers, they began to observe stricter safety measures.[100]

Boiled down, prevention was the responsibility of the employee.[101] If an injury occurred on the job, the company rarely if ever took steps to make things right. If one worker was injured to the point of incapacity, there was always someone else to step in. But that began to change as labor unions grew in Frog Hollow's factories and legislators passed worker-friendly protections, since "the workingman is the one least able to bear the burden of liability."[102]

For decades Travelers owned the market on accident insurance, and by 1885 the company announced it had sold one million policies, an astonishingly high number, considering the fairly restrictive rules that dictated who could be covered. Only men between the ages of eighteen and seventy (who were considered employable) could be insured. Women were uninsurable, as were people without jobs, because their time was considered statistically worthless.[103] Policies were written to provide compensation in the event of the death of the policyholder, or the loss of two limbs, the loss of eyesight, or the loss of one limb and one eye, or any combination thereof.[104]

The rules changed as more women entered the factories. By 1900 as many as 50 percent of all U.S. workers—male and female—were covered by some kind of policy that protected against financial ruin in the case of illness.[105] But this industry wasn't based in Frog Hollow. Much of the insurance business was downtown or just to the north of the neighborhood, in graceful Asylum Hill. The insurance industry would carry Hartford through financially lean times, but by the 1960s all that remained of Frog Hollow's manufacturing powerhouse was shells of factories surrounded by sturdy Perfect Six apartments. In those dwellings the doors shut tight, the walls were thick, and the stairwells held the smell of garlic, potatoes, and meat from two generations of families. If the factories were gone, the housing remained.

3. *A Dream of Social Order*

THE GOVERNMENT SEGREGATES
A NEIGHBORHOOD

In the 1940s and '50s, the apartment at 530 Park Street was, like so many dwellings in the neighborhood at the time, a cold-water flat. The Vanns, a family that included Anthony, an Italian American, and Anita, whose family was French Canadian, moved in when Tony returned from duty in World War II.

Living without hot water meant that bath times revolved around a routine. Anita Vann would run water in the tub, while Tony, who ran a luncheonette in downtown Hartford and worked as a superintendent for their building, heated kettles of water on the kitchen stove for their two daughters.

One of those daughters, Korky, would be a longtime *Hartford Courant* writer, and her Hartford bona fides are securely in place. Korky's mother had gone to the neighborhood's St. Anne's School, where French was spoken as much as English. Korky Vann attended school there herself. Her grandfather worked at Royal Typewriter, and her grandmother was a furrier in downtown Hartford.

St. Anne's was the center of Korky Vann's universe, along with the French Social Club. She remembers speaking French as a girl. Though she's mostly lost that skill to atrophy, the sound of a French Canadian accent still sends her off on a nostalgic wave.

When she was in the fourth grade, Vann's family moved west to Washington Street, near Ward, and she attended Immaculate Conception School. After school she would go to the Mitchell House on Lawrence, a popular neighborhood center that was part of a social settlement movement that began in Hartford in the 1870s.

Back then, women like Elizabeth Colt, Samuel Colt's widow, made it their business to provide for what were often called the street urchins of the city. Though school attendance was mandatory, movers and shakers worried that some immigrant families weren't as keen on education as they were on putting their children to work to help supplement the family income. The idea was to provide activities, from English to cooking classes, to help students assimilate. For Vann, the center offered after-school activities. It also offered adult education classes.

She remembers a vibrant Frog Hollow that was sufficient to any family's needs: a grocery store, a movie theater (the Lyric), two five-and-dimes, and a robust library. As soon as she could write her name, Vann got a library card. "That was great motivation," she said. "You didn't need to travel far outside for what you needed day to day." Frog Hollow kids went ice-skating at Pope Park in the winter and watched fireworks there in the summer. The world ended at the end of her street.

For the Vanns, education was paramount. Both girls went to college. When her parents bought a small cottage on the Connecticut shore, they knew they were living the American Dream, Vann said.

Frog Hollow has been a laboratory, not just for manufacturers but for housing and urban policies as well. Not all of those policies worked to better the neighborhood. Attempts to socially engineer the place often fell far short of the ideal. From an odd plan to move residents out to a city created especially for them in eastern Connecticut to blatantly racist redlining, Frog Hollow has been the guinea pig for multiple attempts to improve the neighborhood—without the manufacturing base it was built around.

Housing has always been fundamental to the American Dream. Early factory owners knew that. Colonel Pope planned a workers' village with two hundred graceful homes, all within walking distance of his twenty-four-hour factories. There would be townhouses and parks and roundabouts and, of course, paved roads for his bicycles and later for Pope automobiles. Pope eventually doubled the size of his planned settlement to four hundred homes, but when the city of Hartford could not come up with enough financial support, the development was scrapped.[1]

If that large a development was an overreach, scattered-site factory housing was common throughout Frog Hollow. Housing for midlevel managers was built on Columbia Street, off of Capitol Avenue, with a line of attached, three-story, single-family houses. The twelve homes on the west side were built in 1888, and the east side was built a year later. Like so many of Hartford's more memorable structures, the homes were designed by Keller, and Columbia is considered one of the prettiest streets in the capital city. Pope's motivation for creating factory housing wasn't just for the convenience of his workers. He said: "Contented labor emigrates with hesitation. . . . When they get a man who looks for a garden at the start, that man is permanent . . . the little garden is a loadstone to the higher nature of him who works hard, and can only get a few minutes in the twilight or at early dawn to drink in what little Nature has set before him, but which is his own."[2] He also offered employees a hot lunch and a two-week vacation every year, though as was common, workers were not paid during the time they took for vacation.

Publications of the day insisted Pope's factory complex was the standard by which all other manufacturers should be measured. In fact, Pope was simply following in the footsteps of other successful factory owners, such as Samuel Colt. Before he died of gout in 1862, Colt, according to David Radcliffe in *Charter Oak Terrace: Life, Death, and Rebirth of a Public Housing Project*, built the nation's first war-related housing when he constructed thirty wooden homes in the city's South Meadows area for his employees. Other employers, if they wanted to keep their workforce happy, had to follow suit. Even before Pope rode in on his bicycle, the neighborhood's first company row houses were laid out, in 1873, along Babcock Street, named for the colonial family that ran the *American Mercury*.

A walk through the neighborhood is far more interesting when the stroller is armed with a little historical context. At the end of the 1700s, what later became Capitol Avenue was a dirt lane that emptied into pastures west of town.[3] A petition granted by the General Assembly on May 29, 1784, set the city boundaries from the Connecticut River to what is now the corner of Washington and Jefferson streets, and then roughly to the corner of Lafayette and Park streets. The same charter called for a mayor, aldermen, and a common council to meet annually. They would be empowered to, among other activities, "lay out new highways, streets, and public walks, and to alter those already laid out, to exchange highways for highways, and to sell highways for the purpose of buying others."[4]

Neighborhoods such as Frog Hollow tended to be fairly self-contained, but as the city expanded so did its public transportation system. A trolley system began to snake its way through Frog Hollow. By the turn of the last century, more than one hundred cars passed in front of downtown's city hall every hour, and electric lines went from the city hall to Pope Park, up Zion Street, and over by New Park Avenue. A car went by every ten minutes and fares cost pennies.

In addition to rows of Perfect Sixes, pavement came to the neighborhood in 1916. The pavement's arrival was long anticipated, but the process of installation tested business owners' patience. Frog Hollow was known for a lot of things, but mostly it was known as the muddiest section of town. The ghost of Dolly Babcock's well seemed ready to assert itself at any time with ground that would inexplicably give way to a bubbling underground stream. Residents sometimes woke up to small ponds in their yards, the result of overnight settling.

Street improvement came after much discussion as to how the "new-fangled pavement" would affect horses and their owners. One *Courant* letter writer in 1901 was opposed to the traditional macadam on city streets: "No calk [*sic*] yet invited will support a horse on this pavement when there is a thin coating of ice upon it," and a smoother surface meant that pedestrians would have to summon even more courage when crossing the street, thus putting the onus on the horse driver to make sure not to run them down.[5]

Residents soon found out that pavement wasn't the issue. The danger in the neighborhood was the addition of those trolleys. The Hartford police department added a twelve-person traffic squad after a traffic death downtown in July 1905. A woman had stepped off a trolley car directly into the line of another car. That death was particularly gruesome, but the newspapers were full of stories of serious injuries resulting from encounters with trolleys, including lost limbs and life-altering head injuries, and each report of a trolley incident was followed by letters decrying the too-fast pace of modernity. Members of the new traffic squad ushered in a small sense of security to a neighborhood that was increasingly becoming a tangle of trolley lines and overhead wires.

"In a sense, traffic officers are born, they are not made," said a 1915 *Courant* feature story on the group. "The men must have qualities not possessed by the average member of the force," including confidence and steely nerves.[6]

Those skills would serve officers well in a neighborhood that sometimes bristled with racial tension. African Americans who moved north to work in the tobacco fields also looked for work in the hollow's factories. But while the police force was watching over a neighborhood that was relatively racially diverse, that would change as factories grew and housing for (overwhelmingly white) blue-collar workers went for a premium. Over time, black residents began to leave the hollow for houses in the north end of Hartford, which remains roughly 64 percent African American and 31 percent Hispanic. They did not necessarily move by choice. Public policy, unspoken and otherwise, pushed them out.

The creation of the Federal Housing Administration (FHA) in 1934—lauded for making home ownership accessible—helped dig deep moats around certain neighborhoods, including Frog Hollow.[7] This was the birth of redlining, the use of discriminatory banking, insurance, and lending practices that keep certain people from climbing up the ladder and out. In Frog Hollow those people included African Americans, some of whom had been in the area since colonial times, and recent immigrants. The federal government would not insure mortgages in neighborhoods like Frog Hollow.[8]

The housing bubble of the 1920s and then the Great Depression had turned bankers into conservative lenders. Something was needed to loosen the purse strings after home ownership sunk to 44 percent nationwide—and substantially less in urban areas such as Hartford.[9] Mortgage rates hovered around 7 percent. Would-be buyers were expected to put down half the cost of the home, and generally mortgage loans were due within five years.[10] Created by the National Housing Act of 1934, the Federal Housing Administration was meant to bolster the stagnant housing market of the early '30s.[11] It did that, but mostly only for white people.

As rural southern African Americans headed north to the factories and immigrants settled in Frog Hollow, a federal organization called the Home Owners' Loan Corporation published a map that ranked Hartford's neighborhoods on a scale of A to D. Neighborhoods that examiners believed would be peopled with residents likely to repay

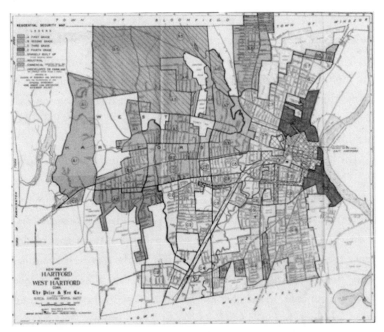

Residential Security Map of Hartford Area 1937, Home Owners' Loan
Corporation. Records of the Federal Home Loan Bank Board, National
Archives II, College Park, Maryland. Retrieved from "On the Line: How
Schooling, Housing, and Civil Rights Shaped Hartford and Its Suburbs,"
https://ontheline.trincoll.edu/book/

a mortgage were marked "A." Neighborhoods that were considered
riskier for mortgage defaults were rated "D" (and colored red on
the map). The HOLC was trying to judge the desirability of neighborhoods in more than two hundred cities around the country so
that the Federal Home Loan Bank could make decisions on which
mortgages could be viable.[12]

The effect on neighborhoods was instantaneous, and it didn't stop
after the Depression. In fact, old redlining maps served as a harbinger
of the devastation to come. Neighborhoods where mortgages were

not backed were—and are—neighborhoods that remain economically vulnerable. Researchers at a University of North Carolina interdisciplinary group took old FHA redlining maps and laid them over the modern-day maps of certain cities in California. Their website shows that the effects of redlining remain.[13] The discrimination that was codified in federal policy indelibly and adversely affected those neighborhoods.

The bulk of Frog Hollow was rated "C," the next-to-lowest ranking. One appraisal report described the land as "slightly rolling," and favorable influences included "nearness to places of employment." However, the buildings, said the report, were older and business and industry were encroaching into residential areas. As for the inhabitants, most were factory workers, according to the report; the families were "mixed" racially and the number of "relief families" was "quite a few." The report said the neighborhood was "very old and congested" and suggested that lenders should "exercise utmost caution."[14] From the 1937 map, green-tinted "A" areas—the highest ranking—were nonexistent in Hartford, though there were a few scattered blue (B) areas in the extreme north and south ends of the city.

The corporation ranked blocks with larger minority populations with a "D" as the riskiest neighborhoods for issuing mortgages. Even the presence of a small number of minority families could drop the ranking of a neighborhood to a "C." Defaults were assumed to be most likely where people of color lived. The effect was the equivalent of shutting the door on black home ownership. As those rent neighborhoods deteriorated, residents who could afford to began to move to the suburbs, taking with them their taxes and support of local schools.[15]

Meanwhile, the former Hartford residents who had moved to the suburbs pulled the rope up after themselves by writing racist covenants that excluded black residents, thereby pushing suburban dwelling even further out of reach and consigning generations of families of color to low-resource neighborhoods. The Federal Housing Administration, while encouraging more home ownership, allowed illegal restrictions on mortgages in favor of whites. In 1955 one writer said: "From its inception the FHA set itself up as the protector of the all white neighborhood. It sent its agents into the field to keep Negroes and other minorities from buying houses in white neighborhoods. It exerted pressure against builders who dared to build for minorities, and against lenders willing to lend on mortgages."[16]

After redlining and withholding resources from vulnerable neighborhoods, the FHA called for restrictive covenants in the suburbs that helped keep neighborhoods homogenous—and white. Racial or ethnic mixing was considered "undesirable encroachment."[17] The FHA protected "all-white neighborhoods" and its field agents were charged with keeping "Negroes and other minorities from buying houses in white neighborhoods."[18] What had been a relatively integrated city became divided strictly by race, and then again by class.[19] All this happened with the support of—in fact, the blessing of—the federal government.

By this point, the Frog Hollow neighborhood had peaked in population, and the apartments that had been home to factory workers stood empty. And then the Japanese attacked Pearl Harbor. Prior to December 1941, city officials polled personnel managers, who all said that Hartford needed more housing for its workers. Though manufacturing was moving elsewhere, the town continued to grow from a population of 138,000 in 1920 to 165,000 in 1930. The immigration wave slowed, but southern African Americans were streaming into the city.

Once the United States declared war, government officials scrambled to provide temporary housing until more permanent homes could be built. The ground was laid for such housing—literally—by the U.S. Public Housing Act of 1937. The act's original intent was to place the creation of housing under the purview of the federal government, but cities insisted they knew best what their residents needed. Local housing authorities were created to form plans for much-needed affordable homes.[20]

During World War II, the housing projects around Hartford—places such as Nelton Court, Charter Oak, and Rice Heights—were hastily built as temporary housing for defense workers, though they did include amenities such as playgrounds, community centers, and health clinics. Originally, the projects were meant to include mixed-income housing, where middle-class and economically struggling families would live side by side. The intent was to help working-class families, the "submerged middle class" whose fortunes had been sunk by the Great Depression. One of the authors of the bill, Robert Wagner, a longtime senator from New York, said, "There are some whom we cannot expect to serve, those who cannot pay rent."[21] The bill was supposed to reduce the slums of the cities, which in Hartford were clustered around neighborhoods like Frog Hollow. The act was supposed to open the door for all, according to Catherine Bauer, housing expert and urban planner.[22] It was the government's first attempt to address housing needs for low- and moderate-income families. (Other attempts would come after World War II, during the late 1960s and into the '70s under President Richard Nixon.[23]) A postwar lobbying effort to stymie mixed-income development successfully ended that dream.

In Connecticut the answer to a lack of housing during World War II was projects such as the 137-acre Charter Oak Terrace. When it was finished in 1942, the project included fifteen miles of sewer lines and forty miles of pipes, a library, a basketball court, and morning glories climbing up trellises, according to the *Courant*. People had been living in trailer camps and tobacco sheds and in crumbling Perfect Sixes around Frog Hollow. At the time, the prevailing concern in housing was not affordability but that so many of the structures were substandard. Outhouses were common, as were cold-water flats.[24]

The Hartford Housing Authority expected the project structures to last at least sixty years. To qualify for a spot in the project, a family's head of household had to work in the defense industry. Seventeen hundred applicants signed up for one thousand units. Despite the utilitarian nature of the project, this was a step up for some of the employees.

By 1942 Hartford was one of 290 communities with a total of 175,000 public housing apartments, built mostly to house defense industry workers.[25] A 1942 yearbook published by the National Association of Housing Officials said that these houses served two purposes:

1. They provided shelter in critical defense or war production areas, and
2. They contributed to the rehabilitation of blighted urban areas.[26]

By 1943 Connecticut was home to roughly half of all the government war housing built in New England, and half of that could be found in the Hartford–New Britain area.[27] The *Courant* reported that four hundred new housing units—in addition to the some eight thousand already developed—were being added for "white in-migrant families," while African Americans drawn to the capital city were housed in "temporary dormitories."[28] Berkeley Cox, an Oregon native and former law professor who was chairman of the Hartford Housing Authority at the time, assured the newspaper that this arrangement was entirely satisfactory to all parties. If there was an attempt to ask this to an African American living in a temporary dormitory—and eighteen thousand of them moved to Connecticut during World War II—a response was not recorded.[29]

In some areas of the country, particularly San Francisco, mobile homes barely had a chance to establish themselves as recreational vehicles before they became the answer to an acute lack of wartime housing. Everywhere cities were scrambling to find housing.[30] In

Frog Hollow the Perfect Sixes that had decreased in value quickly filled.

After the war, real estate lobbyists, among others, pushed to restrict renting public housing to low-income families only. This too helped codify the segregation of American cities such as Hartford and American neighborhoods such as Frog Hollow.[31] Twenty years after she praised public housing, Catherine Bauer wrote that low-rent housing "still drags along in a kind of limbo, continuously controversial, not dead but never more than half alive."[32]

When the war ended, Charter Oak transformed itself into a subsidized housing project. Another project, Rice Heights, on a former dairy farm, was built specifically for veterans, but developers used inferior products and residents complained about a host of issues with their units. In 1955 an epic flood damaged the already-deteriorating project even more. A few families who had lived through Frog Hollow's industrial powerhouse days held on to their apartments, but the push was to move to the suburbs and leave Hartford behind.

The state legislature appointed a ten-member Inter-Racial Commission in July 1943 to listen to complaints about discrimination in housing, and in their 1950 report the commission said that "wherever discrimination or inequities existed, Negroes invariably were the recipients."[33] Only Rice Heights was listed as an example of a successfully integrated housing project. The project was considered so noteworthy that on the basis of its success, the New Haven Housing Authority began to integrate its own projects.

Nowhere was the suburb siren louder than in neighborhoods such as Frog Hollow. Suburbs were not new, but access to them via mass transportation and highways was. Newly paved roads allowed middle-class neighborhood residents to live away from their workplace.

For generations in the Hartford area, blue-collar workers tended to remain close to their workplaces, while more affluent employees could afford to pay for transportation that would take them some distance between work and home. Originally, according to Robert Fishman in "Bourgeois Utopias: The Rise and Fall of Suburbia," the assumption was that the wealthier city residents lived and worked at the center of town, while the people with fewer resources were pushed farther out. But then, at the time, home and work were virtually one and the same.[34]

At the onset of suburbs, this often meant that white, better-paid workers formed these new small towns that served as feeder communities to the larger cities in their midst. As automobiles became more plentiful and relatively more affordable, more city dwellers could opt out of city living for that white picket fence. Car ownership across the United States went from 60 percent in 1940 to 80 percent in 1960.

In Hartford, city residents began shifting outward. Sometimes they were following their employers, and sometimes employers were following worker migration, or attractive tax breaks. In 1929 Pratt & Whitney moved across the Connecticut River to East Hartford, where the workforce focused on building aircraft engines.

The advent of highways to whisk workers to and from work did not serve Frog Hollow particularly well. Joseph F. DiMento, a law professor at the University of California, Irvine, has studied the effect of highways on midsized cities. In Syracuse, DiMento said the policy of building highways to avoid urban congestion helped contribute to the death of urban neighborhoods and the rise of "racially motivated segregation."[35] That same effect could be seen in Hartford, where city planners responded to the 1944 Federal Aid Highway Act, which offered federal money for construction costs of highways. Highway construction went into high gear under President Dwight Eisenhower, who supported the program as a boon to commerce, national security, and unity among the states.[36] In December 1944, with the passage of the Federal Aid Highway Act, the state began planning three highways, including what would become I-84, I-91, and I-95. Construction on I-84 started in the western part of the state in 1958.

The east-west highway, including a stretch through Hartford, began to open in sections three years later.[37]

Transportation in the nineteenth century—railroads—pushed population into the most remote parts of the country. Highways reduced the "friction of space," with vehicles that could pull cities toward remote areas.[38] According to Alana Semuels, a writer for *Atlantic* magazine, policymakers looked at cities as doctors looked at human bodies. Cities had disease. They needed cures. And policymakers considered one city a cookie-cutter version of the next.[39] That approach was disastrous for cities like Hartford.

When planned properly highways are like arteries and veins that keep a body healthy, but to build them some neighborhoods must be sacrificed. In many cases, those neighborhoods were the ones that were the most economically challenged. This left residents crowded into increasingly blighted areas, some of which were unfit for human habitation.

The suburban exodus was as impressive as the industrialization of a few years earlier. In rather short order, suburbanites outnumbered people living in the cities. Frog Hollow apartment houses filled with new families of new ethnicities, and a block-long brick building at the corner of Capitol and Flower—which included the original home of Pratt & Whitney Co.'s small tool division—was all that remained of the vast industrial complex.

There were all kinds of reasons to leave. Much like the earlier goldmines playing out in the western part of the country, Hartford had a feel of being played out. Manufacturers were leaving and consolidating elsewhere. Affordable homes—with yards and more privacy—were becoming available in far-off Manchester and Windsor. If the American Dream beckoned, it beckoned from outside the city limits.

Meanwhile, Frog Hollow's manufacturing base kept shrinking. Between 1963 and 1972 Hartford lost 26,400 jobs, 36 percent of all the jobs in the city.[40] People who'd left Hartford for inner suburbs such as East Hartford or Bloomfield were now pushing farther out to the rural towns of Stafford and Canton.[41]

Something had to give. Tensions in Frog Hollow culminated with violent riots in 1967 and 1969. An elderly Puerto Rican man was attacked by a motorcycle gang whose members had been harassing Hispanics and Latinos in town. Riots became so prevalent that in June 1969 a citywide curfew was imposed. During one particularly violent weekend, police arrested vanloads of Frog Hollow's Puerto Rican residents, and the Puerto Ricans—not all of whom had been rioting—reacted angrily. They were the victims of attacks, they said, yet the police handcuffed and arrested them. Bottles were thrown and windows smashed as rioting continued for four days. Police retaliated by tear-gassing crowds. Maria Clemencia Colón Sánchez, then the only Puerto Rican member of the Hartford Democratic Town Committee, suggested a meeting between city officials and the Puerto Rican community. At first the offer was rebuffed by the city's white powerbrokers. Elisha Freedman, then the city manager, insisted to the *Hartford Times* newspaper that the discussion would best be conducted through already-existing neighborhood organizations.

To the residents, that statement indicated a lack of commitment by city officials to work with the Latino/Hispanic communities and to help people living in increasingly impoverished areas. His remarks also exemplified the poor relations between town officials and the roughly twenty thousand Puerto Ricans who lived in town, most of them in Frog Hollow. The residents wanted to talk about substandard housing and the treatment by police of Hartford's residents of color. Freedman and others, including Thomas J. Vaughan, then Hartford's police chief, eventually met with the town residents, but their meeting only briefly interrupted the riots. For Frog Hollow, that was the beginning of a tradition of meetings that went nowhere, riots that broke windows, and eventually a Puerto Rican community that began to organize.

Meanwhile, other parts of Hartford were enjoying new construction, and the contrast between the attention paid to, say, the downtown area versus that paid to neighborhoods like Frog Hollow (and Clay-Arsenal and Asylum Hill) was stunning. In a 1988 essay Kenneth J. Neubeck and Richard E. Ratcliff wrote: "On weekdays the downtown resembles the new service-oriented, post-industrial society often proclaimed to be the bright future of the United States. However, the close of the business day brings another side of Hartford into view. As downtown workers pour out of buildings, most heading for homes in the suburbs, left behind is a central city whose residential population is disproportionately poor and minority."[42]

Frog Hollow continued its predictable, preventable downward spiral. The rapid decline that started in the 1960s and continued through the early '70s had slowed, wrote Neubeck and Ratcliff, but Frog Hollow was still deteriorating. To counter the decline, city leaders decided to dip their toe into some social engineering. After decades of inattention, city movers and shakers decided to manipulate "environmental and social forces to create a high probability that effective social action" would occur.[43] Arthur J. Lumsden, Greater Hartford Chamber of Commerce president, convinced business leaders that the quality of life in the city desperately needed preserving, and that they should play a role in that preservation. Executives from United Aircraft, Connecticut General Life Insurance, Aetna Life and Casualty, and Travelers Insurance as well as labor leaders and others formed a group called the Greater Hartford Community Development Corporation.[44] It was big and well funded, and its members were willing to think regionally after generations of strict hometown rule.

Forty staff members published a 150-page plan called the Hartford Process in 1972.[45] The Process (as it became known) was far-reaching and innovative, and implementation would take fifteen years, eight hundred million dollars, and massive amounts of political will.[46] The

Arthur J. Lumsden, former president of the Greater Hartford Chamber of Commerce in his Hartford office. December 12, 1983. Photo by Michael McAndrews. Courtesy of the *Hartford Courant*

plan called for moving families from certain struggling neighborhoods to a proposed new community in Coventry, Conn., a rural town about a half hour east of Hartford. Profits from the new town would help fund the revitalization of places like Frog Hollow.[47]

Social engineering was not a new concept, certainly not in Hartford. Industrial housing in Frog Hollow? Social engineering. Highways to move people in and out of the city? Social engineering. Sidewalks that separated pedalers and playing children from traffic? Also social engineering. But the Process went too far.

A memo from the Process appeared in the local press that called for ghettoes to be moved away from the downtown. José Cruz, in his 2010 book *Identity and Power: Puerto Rican Politics and the Challenge of Ethnicity*, said that Eugenio Caro, who had worked for the Hartford police department before he worked briefly for the Process, shared the memo with La Casa de Puerto Rico, whose members then shared it with the press.[48]

The gist of the plan was that Bellevue Square would be torn down. The western part of Frog Hollow, along with other neighborhoods, would be rehabilitated. "We must," the memo said, "manage the population mix in those areas, including *selective relocation* to keep welfare population below 15–20 percent."[49] The memo also called for Puerto Rican in-migration to be reduced and said that "efforts should be made to consolidate the welfare dependent elements of this population in Clay Hill and eastern Frog Hollow, using Section 8 rehab to provide relocation resources in these areas and in the suburbs."[50]

Neighborhood residents sensed that the plan was strictly a means of removing them from Hartford and they had no trust that they would benefit from "selective relocation." And so they resisted. They were joined by some suburban allies, and together the groups rallied. In January 1975 the group came downtown to protest, and later that year the plan was scraped for "economic reasons."[51]

No one argued in favor of stasis. No one—business titans, city residents, or suburban residents—benefited from Hartford's slow demise. But change organized and created by people who don't live in Hartford has a way of not working. Change had to come from within.

In 1979 the Frog Hollow neighborhood was listed on the National Register of Historic Places for its preservation of a pristine working-class neighborhood. The neighborhood, according to the citation, was "an urban scene with unity of mass and scale which gives a remarkable sense of place." It had also been blessedly overlooked by the urban renewal push of the 1950s and '60s, when Hartford saw the construction of Constitution Plaza, a 3.8-acre development of six buildings and a parking garage near the Connecticut River. That futuristic complex replaced an area known as Front Street, whose decaying tenements were damaged from years of flooding and neglect. For years the plaza was a popular spot around the winter holidays, with its lights and Santa Claus arriving in a helicopter. Ironically, urban renewal skipped Frog Hollow. No one had looked at the neighborhood as a candidate for improvement. One architectural study of the neighborhood called it "undistinguished" but said the buildings "do provide an excellent, well-preserved example" of some of Hartford's best architecture. The neighborhood's lack of distinction protected the graceful, turn-of-the-century brick apartments and storefronts from sometimes well-meaning but misguided "renewal."

Meanwhile, the city's stock of decent, affordable housing was shrinking. More and more, "affordable" meant "substandard." Factory housing built at the turn of the century was in need of repair, but landlords were increasingly resistant to modernization. They knew there would always be families willing to live in the most dilapidated apartments. With the manufacturing core of the city moved to East Hartford, West Hartford, and beyond—and highways built to take employees to those new factories—the city still had housing but gone were the well-paying jobs of the previous generation. In 1960 about half of Hartford's 116,000 workers lived in the city. By 1980 there were twice as many jobs but less than a quarter of the people who worked in Hartford lived there.[52]

While the city barely invested in public housing, the public housing that existed was aging. Charter Oak Terrace was crumbling.[53] Homeownership plummeted until roughly 75 percent of Hartford's residents were renters, and the majority of them were renting from absentee landlords.

The result was a segregated Hartford that served as a magnet for more segregation. Poverty began to attract poverty to Frog Hollow. Elsewhere in the nation, home ownership doubled between 1940 and 1980.[54] That pillar of the American Dream crumbled in Frog Hollow. While other families were enjoying the stability and the capital accumulation that come with home ownership, families in Frog Hollow were bedding down in increasingly ramshackle Perfect Sixes.

Advocates called the growing tide a perfect storm of bad public policy and rough luck. In the Reagan years, federal assistance programs that had helped keep people housed and fed were cut, while military spending increased. As an example, President Reagan cut in half the budget for public housing and subsidized Section 8 housing. While units of low-income housing shrank, the population of people who were homeless soared—to 1.2 million by the late 1980s.[55] Government policy turned the former shelter society into a shelter industry.[56]

If industry was gone, work in the tobacco fields still called African Americans and Hispanics to the Hartford area, and many moved to the north end of the city closer to the fields. In Puerto Rico the government was encouraging immigration to the mainland to ease overpopulation on the island.[57] Meanwhile, the new Department of Labor was negotiating agreements between Puerto Rico and industries in Connecticut.[58]

There were other, more visible signs that the neighborhood was struggling, including an increase of men, mostly young, living on the streets. In the winter of 1981 a young boy ran into Immaculate Conception Church and insisted that Father James M. Donagher follow him outside. "Father! Come!" the boy said. The priest did, down an alley to the frozen body of a young man leaning against a stoop at the rear of a building. It was two days after Christmas. The man came from a prominent family in Mexico, but he drank, Donagher said. Unable to imagine anyone else freezing to death, Father Donagher, who died in 2016, opened the basement of the church the next night to anyone who needed shelter. Though Donagher hadn't asked for permission or applied for permits, the archbishop funded the endeavor, although he constantly reminded Donagher that had he asked for permission, the answer would have been no. City officials threatened

Father James M. Donagher.
Author photo

to close the shelter, but Donagher stood firm. Thus began a shelter
that would become ImmaCare Inc., an organization that included
Casa de Francisco, a fifty-unit supportive housing complex.[59]

Other shelters opened in other parts of Hartford as the homeless
population swelled. Down Main Street, South Park Inn opened
in 1982, also in an old church. While federal programs were being
slashed in Washington, Connecticut was facing a significant budget
deficit, and the state hired consultants to figure a way through the
crisis. The recommendation, contained in the Thomas Commission
report, suggested closing two of the state's four mental hospitals, at a
savings of about thirty-one million dollars.[60] Advocates had sought
to deinstitutionalize people with mental illness since the 1950s, but
some housing advocates cried foul. Care in the hospitals wasn't always
up to par, but the places at least supplied a bed. In many cases, family
support was exhausted or nonexistent. Without the hospitals, many
people with significant mental illness would be homeless.

All the while, housing costs were rising and cities, bent on urban
renewal, were tearing down traditional last stops for people who
couldn't afford conventional housing: single-room occupancy hotels,
or SROS. In Connecticut the state was closing or shrinking the number of beds at state hospitals. When they were gone, a large cohort

of people was left without any options but the street. Immaculate Conception and other organizations like it became their last stop.

Today Frog Hollow is overwhelmingly renter occupied (93.6 percent), and half of those renters are spending more than 35 percent of their monthly income on rent. This is problematic on several levels. The Department of Housing and Urban Development suggests that families pay no more than 30 percent of their household income on housing. According to that line of thinking, if a family is paying more than 30 percent for rent or mortgage, then something else goes wanting—perhaps adequate food, or education.[61]

The neighborhood's housing market is also characterized by transience: 79 percent of the population in Frog Hollow has moved at least once in the past five years, with the attendant disruption that creates in a child's education. As is often the case, the smallest residents were left to deal with the effects of disruption that had long been a part of Frog Hollow.

4. The Fullest Stature

ORIGINAL RESIDENTS ARE PUSHED OUT,

THE NEIGHBORHOOD GETS A REPUTATION—

AND EVERYONE IS BASEBALL CRAZY

In April 1909 a widow named Emily Brown couldn't pay the rent at her flat at 367 Park Street, and her landlord, William Solomon, was done waiting. An eviction notice arrived at 5:30 on a rainy evening, and without much ceremony—or recorded protest from Mrs. Brown—the widow's possessions were moved to the curb. Despite the rain, Widow Brown sat in a chair with her goods around her until a passerby offered to buy her furniture. Sensing a way out of her financial mess, Mrs. Brown announced that she would sell everything. The crowd that gathered soon stretched out into the street, and a police officer came to direct traffic—and keep neighborhood boys from stealing Mrs. Brown's worldly possessions. A peddler soon arrived and offered to buy everything for fifty dollars, but a neighbor interrupted to say Mrs. Brown could make more money selling her goods piece by piece.

The *Courant* article from April 14, 1909, reads like a ledger: a workman bought a sewing machine for seven dollars. (Whether the machine was a Weed is lost to the ages.) A large cook stove went for nine dollars. By 9 p.m. Mrs. Brown was tired and she had to lower herself onto a nearby doorstop, as her chair was in the possession of a new owner. Volunteers carried the leftover furniture to the corner of Park and Putnam and left it in a pile. Someone fetched a canvas to cover what remained of her worldly goods, and Mrs. Brown went to the grocery store with thirty dollars. She decided to go to her daughter's house in Hartford for the night and left, even when a woman in a nightgown ran up crying, "Mrs. Brown, Mrs. Brown, have you got a refrigerator to sell?" The article ended: "Mrs. Brown, however, remained firm in her resolve to call the sale off for the night and kept on. . . . Family photographs and other relics that cannot be replaced were left strewn in the gutter."

Had Mrs. Brown hit her financial shoals ten years later, a new state pension fund might have helped her. In its first year the fund rescued twenty such widows in Hartford with monthly settlements. Only native-born widows were eligible.[1]

On a larger scale, Mrs. Brown's Frog Hollow denouement might serve as a metaphor for the neighborhood. Frog Hollow was approaching its pinnacle, and it would be—not to put too fine a point on it—mostly downhill from there, in terms of production and development. The streets would see no more major building, and within a couple of decades the same unprecedented growth in those few blocks would occur in reverse, as if someone was running a film backward. Decade by decade the town, and the neighborhood, shrank. Survival in the neighborhood began to mean making enough money to move out.

As people moved away, Frog Hollow attracted some of the city's more rough-and-tumble residents, and those residents—immigrants and native-born alike—had a reputation for scrappiness and a keen sense of survival. That's a reputation that continues today.

The *Courant* ran a story on December 28, 1915, with the headline "Frog Hollow Bunch in Street Fight." Four young Frog Hollow men were arrested after a "spectacular free-for-all" that started at about 1 a.m. in front of the Bond Hotel to the east of the neighborhood.

Hartford's Population, 1910–2010

YEAR	POPULATION OF HARTFORD
1910	98,915
1920	138,036
1930	164,072
1940	166,267
1950	177,397
1960	162,178
1970	158,017
1980	136,392
1990	139,739
2000	121,578
2010	124,775

Source: U.S. Census Bureau.

Two were charged with public drunkenness and two with breach of the peace—just another day in the crowded, rollicking neighborhood. Police officers hated to break up fights in and around the hollow, because the responsibility of hauling the miscreants to the station (usually on foot) fell on individual law enforcement officers. If someone didn't happen by with a wagon or carriage, the police officer would have to fight the entire way.

James Francis Lally was a Hartford cop who lived in the neighborhood on Laurel Street. Lally had been born in County Westmeath in central Ireland and had run off as a boy to New York City. He'd moved on to Hartford and served in the navy with his brother, John. They'd both served on the USS *Monitor,* where John had been killed in front of James. James had come home to work as an engineer on the railroads, but he became a police officer at age forty-one. On the force he was known, according to his 1906 obituary, for his ability to "straighten out the 'plug uglies' of Frog Hollow." The neighborhood had an abundance of both plugs and uglies.

Despite the continual shifts in culture and climate, Frog Hollow retained a small-town feel. In the early 1900s, when a firefighter at Engine Co. No. 6 lost his black and tan dog, he put the word out up and down Park Street because, according to a *Courant* story of the day, "children in the hollow are sad." The neighborhood had grown because of abundant manufacturing jobs. The neighborhood shrank as those jobs moved elsewhere.

But always there was plenty of water, and this had drawn not only the manufacturers but the earliest settlers before them. Imagine black dirt fed by abundant streams, and a rolling meadow marked by heavily traveled trails. Frog Hollow's original inhabitants were drawn to the hollow's water, to what would later be called the Connecticut River and to the many small tributaries that laced the land known as Suckiaug. Alternately spelled "Sicaog," "Sicoag," Suckiag," and "Saukiog," it is an Algonquin word used to describe black, fertile river bottomland.

There weren't many people of Suckiaug, and they lived in a relatively small space, but historians say the land must have offered something special to pull the natives from the more resource-abundant Long Island Sound. Either the land was in fact special, or the small tribe, with a limited ability to control larger tracts of land, was stuck with the not-so-attractive area that would become Hartford. Whatever their reason for being there, the area played a pivotal role in the region. Native trails allowed early dwellers to come to the site's important cultural events. Perhaps because it was centrally located, Suckiaug was the site of a "hub of activity" for natives.[2]

In 1614 Adrien Block sailed up the Connecticut River in a vessel named *Onrust*, Dutch for "restless." From that thirty-eight-foot vessel, Block saw large villages surrounded by maize fields in the land between Middletown and Hartford.[3] Sequassen, the sachem of the tribe living in the area, the Suckiaug, appears to have welcomed Dutch trade, which may have been a bit of diplomacy on his part.[4] We cannot know for sure. Much of the history of the Hartford area natives has been lost, perhaps because their culture was among the first of the natives' to be annihilated and none of the conquerors thought to take notes. Details of the land transfer vary according to the historian, though in all accounts there is little evidence of a struggle between the peoples.

In the early 1620s Dutch fur traders set up the Fort of Good Hope in an area of Hartford known today as Dutch Point. The original Dutch structure was probably a stockade built around a simple building. Though wood from the site was later poached as landfill, the rest of the site was washed clean by generations of floods, and the original bricks most likely buried under river mud.[5] From an 1899 account of the settlement, the commissary of the post, a Jacob Van Curler, bought from the Pequots an area described as "Suckiage (or black earth)," which was roughly the size of the city of Hartford today, in exchange for "one piece of duffell[1] 27 ells long, 6 axes, 6 kettles, 18 knives, 1 sword-blade, 1 pair of shears, some toys and a musket."[6] That land plot would have included what would later become Frog Hollow.

For nearly twenty years the Dutch used the fort—which stood about a forty-minute walk from present-day Frog Hollow—as an outpost for a way station to send "hundreds of thousands of beaver, otter, mink, and muskrat skins down the river."[7] The land's original residents, in the eyes of their conquerors, set up a "relatively disease-free paradise."[8] According to Roxanne Dunbar-Ortiz, in her 2015 award-winning book, "An Indigenous Peoples' History of the United States," superior medical care and basic hygiene helped keep indigenous peoples healthy. Their mostly vegetarian diet helped as well. The indigenous people of New England had communities and road systems and a mostly agrarian society that was fully functioning long before ships sailed up the Connecticut River. Had such a culture not existed, the Europeans most likely would not have survived their first winter. Only by taking over the plowed land, ready crops, and established roads of the natives could the European settlers have sunk roots and succeeded.

The Great Seal of the State of Connecticut includes a stylized picture of three grapevines (good Christians at work in the vineyard) with the Latin inscription, "*Qui transtulit sustinet,*" or "he who transplanted still sustains."[9] The "transplanted" could refer not so much to the Europeans as to the people the Europeans supplanted in order to grab land.[10]

The natives sold the land around Hartford, according to William De Forest in 1853, "without stint or hesitation."[11] This quiet acquiescence doesn't jibe with the violence in the rest of the state. Historians of the day did think to record the tragic plunder by the English in the southern part of the state. In one May 1637 battle alone, Captain John Mason and his men attacked a village and killed upward of seven hundred Pequots, most of them women and children. By his own account Capt. Mason told his troops that day, "We must burn them," and many of those Pequot women and children were burned alive. Survivors were either sold into slavery in the Caribbean or sent to "praying towns" so that they might convert to Christianity.[12] Praying towns—several of them located in the northeastern part of the state—were the refuges (or prisons) where Christian Indians moved to convert fully to their new religion and culture and to fully renounce their own. Rules in the towns included bans against idleness, bared breasts (for women), and long hair (for men). Infractions were punishable by a fine.[13]

The annihilation of the Pequot tradition was so final that the word *Pequot* was banned by the Treaty of Hartford in 1638. By law, former Pequots were to refer to themselves as Mohegans or Narragansetts.[14] Subsequent historical accounts call the massacre what it was: terrorism.[15]

There are no such recorded massacres for the Hartford area, but the traditional story of local natives cheerfully handing over their land, culture, and livelihoods for a few trinkets stretches the imagination. In fact, in 1657 an alliance of natives and Africans launched a rebellion in Hartford and set fire to some buildings.[16]

When settlers who followed the Reverend Thomas Hooker came to the land after the Dutch, they too went to Sequassen, who was said to have accorded them the kind of welcome he gave the earlier settlers. If the sachem's reaction to the latecomers is accurately portrayed—cautiously cordial—that might have been strategic. The sachem knew his people needed protection from the Mohawks to the west and the Mohegans to the east, and the incoming settlers could provide a well-armed shield, or so he thought. In return, he asked that the English not touch his people's vaunted Charter Oak tree. The Suckiaug used the tree that crowned a hill overlooking the big river as a meeting place for negotiating with other tribes. The tree was also a living calendar. Every season, when the leaves on the tree grew as big as a mouse's ear, the Suckiaug knew it was time for planting.[17] When the English settlers proposed cutting the tree for wood, the natives convinced them to spare it. At the time, they told the English that the tree was at least 760 years old.[18]

The tree, Sequassen told them, was given to them by their great sachem, who had led the tribe from lands out west to the Great (Connecticut) River. Upon planting the tree, Sequassen said, the warriors buried their tomahawks (which they called *tume-hegan*) and settled in to live off the land.[19] Reverence for the tree was passed on to the new settlers. Years later, after a storm blew the tree down in 1856, the *Courant* ran a brief story that decried the fraudulent items purportedly carved from the wood: "Could all the articles which are called Charter

The Charter Oak, 1857, Charles De Wolf Brownell (American, 1822–1909).
Oil on oil canvas, 43⅛ x 54⁵⁄₁₆ in. (109.6 x 138 cm.). Wadsworth Atheneum
Museum of Art, Hartford, Connecticut. Gift of Mrs. Josephine Marshall
Dodge and Marshall Jewell Dodge, in memory of Marshall Jewell, 1898.
Courtesy of Allen Phillips/Wadsworth Atheneum

Oak be collected together, there would be material enough probably
to form a small forest of trees equal in size to the one blown down."[20]

Sequassen sold these English settlers a large area around Hartford
that included what would be the Frog Hollow neighborhood and
stretched west toward the present-day town of Farmington. From an
account written in 1904, the sachem passed the land to the English
in exchange for blankets, coats, and hoes. As with the tribe's other
negotiations, the transfer was made under the Charter Oak.[21]

When settlers moved a few years later to settle the western portion of the land they'd purchased, they paid for the land again.[22] Such multipurchases were not uncommon. Historians say the land around what is now the state's Hammonasset (either "at the place of small islands," or "where we dig") State Beach, forty miles south of Hartford, was purchased no fewer than four different times from the natives living there. Settlers didn't appear to begrudge the transactions. Land in the New World was still cheaper than it would have been in England, and it was far more plentiful. Early deeds were not preserved, but a confirmatory deed in 1670 said the land was given to a Mr. Samuel Stone and a Mr. William Goodwin "in the behalfe of the present proprietors and owners of the lands belonging to the township of Hartford."[23] The town was divided into two townships called "plantations," north and south, with separate record-keeping. The General Court of Connecticut required strict record keeping "fayrely written."[24]

Hooker Walk through the Wilderness, 1636, C. H. Niehaus, 1893.
Connecticut, 1893. Photograph. Retrieved from Library of
Congress, www.loc.gov/item/2004662463/

The Suckiaug were accustomed to compromise. They had been defeated by the Pequots, and Sequassen may have decided that another fight was one fight too many. Though the new settlers promised to leave land free for native trade, the better part of the deal, as with all land transactions between the natives and the English, went to the English. The Dutch and English skirmished over ownership until 1653, when the Dutch mostly moved to New York.

If the land exchange was cordial, in short order the English minimized the role of the Suckiaug with a series of laws that forbade them to own weapons, to enter Hartford as organized groups, or to come into the streets of Hartford at all—individually or as a group—after dark. If the land exchange was peaceful, there existed at least on the part of the English a mistrust of the natives. A later account said that the natives, "though ostensibly friendly, were not to be trusted. Still they pilfered—in dwellings, in the fields, everywhere. They still destroyed swine, seized cattle, and drove off horses. They fired buildings. They might murder"—or so said the settlers, though no such crime wave was ever recorded.[25]

Meanwhile, the new town of Hartford was divided into plots with names such as George Wyllys, Matthew Allyn, Richard Goodman, and John Talcott attached to them. Though settlers came for a new order, the organizers showed a propensity for repeating patterns of their old world. Families whose members had achieved financial success in Great Britain were given more resources in the New World in the form of larger lots. Families unable to contribute as much to the common good were given smaller plots at the "Townes Courtesie."[26]

A 1640 map shows a street marked "from George Steele's to the Great Swamp" that passes through what would be Frog Hollow. Steele, whose will in 1664 included the proviso that his "very best chamber pot" be given to his granddaughter, owned the plot of land at the farthest west point of the road, and the lane stretches toward what is now Frog Hollow.[27] On the 1640 map, Hartford's current

Map of Hartford, Connecticut, c. 1640. Retrieved from New York
Public Library Digital Collections, https://digitalcollections.nypl.org
/items/07171e90-3be8-0134-a6c3-00505686a51c

Main Street is marked "Road from Palisado to Centinel Hill," and its
Front Street near the Connecticut River—the site of so much immigrant activity later—is marked "Windsor to Wethersfield" and "Little
River to North Meadow." The Little Meadow, now roughly the site of
the Connecticut Children's Museum as well as a Marriott, was rich,
tillable land.[28] In fact the land was mostly ready for European occu-

pancy and had been since the Suckiaugs had cleared the brush from the woodlands with strategically set fires. The bottomland was also home to many wetlands, with names like Dead Swamp, Clayboard Swamp, Dry Swamp, and Wet Swamp—a perfect environment for the storied frogs in the hollow.

Streets came to the neighborhood starting in colonial times. One of the earliest paths was known as Malt Lane—now known as Park Street—which most likely got its early name from a malt house located on the property of John Barnard, who migrated from England to Hartford in 1635 with his wife, Mary. As one of the wealthier settlers, Barnard was granted twenty-four acres in the new settlement, including some land in what is now Frog Hollow. Barnard was also among a group of people who called themselves "Adventurers," who preceded the Reverend Hooker, the Cambridge-educated minister who is given credit for founding Connecticut.[29]

The early white settlers were Puritans, which meant they were both literal and literate. For them, God walked the earth, and so did Satan. Puritans were called to be on guard against sin that sometimes took the form of spiritual creatures sent to lead them into iniquity. Though neighboring Massachusetts has the bigger reputation (and attendant modern-day tourism dollars) for witch-hunting, Connecticut was the first to execute someone on charges of sorcery in 1647, nearly fifty years before the Salem witch trials. The first to fall victim to the Connecticut hysteria was Alse (Alice) Young, a Windsor woman who was hanged, probably at what is now the Old State House in downtown Hartford.

Now couple that with the strangely free and easy approach to alcohol among early British settlers. While given to suspicion about their neighbors' potential dealings with the devil, they loved their drink (the purity of the water always a concern). Given the tradition of drinking in British culture, alcohol consumption was as much a part of the Hartford culture as clearing the forest, ratting out the neighbors, and pushing the natives off the land. In fact, by 1770 one estimate put average per capita alcohol consumption in Hartford and elsewhere at 3.7 gallons a year.[30] (Compare that to an annual average of two gallons of alcohol per capita today in the United States, according to the World Health Organization.)[31]

This love affair turned taverns into an almost sacred space for early settlers. Local watering holes were also town centers where people could gossip, perform business, and sometimes even hold court—judicial, that is. In fact, in 1644 the Connecticut colony made taverns mandatory in every town.[32] In 1776 Hartford had twenty-four of them scattered around the town's dirt streets.

This being New England, anything that carried with it the potential for too much fun could not go unregulated. The attitude among the righteous toward demon rum was more relaxed than it would be later, though legislators were anxious to pass laws that punished overimbibers. Drunkenness was still considered a sin, which made the role of beer in colonial America a complicated one. In 1639 a mere five men were arrested and censured for intemperance in Hartford County.[33] That could have meant that people had a high tolerance for alcohol, or that law enforcement was lax.

It might have been the former. A colonist's typical breakfast included a mug of hard cider (also known as small beer). Farmers and others brought their malt to establishments such as John Barnard's for brewing. Since there was no way to transport beer without spoilage, beer was produced and consumed locally.[34]

Later Barnard—once an Adventurer—joined a group of Congregationalists known as Withdrawers, who believed their church was too liberal in matters of baptism and membership.[35] In 1659 Barnard and others asked for a religious hearing, and when the church elders did not support their view, Barnard and others moved north to buy land in Hadley, Mass.[36] There they intended to build the perfect Puritan paradise, with rules aplenty. By the time Hartford was incor-

The Drunkard's Progress, or the Direct Road to Poverty, Wretchedness, and Ruin, designed and published by J. W. Barber of New Haven, Connecticut, 1826. Library of Congress Prints and Photographs Division, Washington, D.C. 20540

porated in 1784, just a corner of Frog Hollow was officially included in the city, around the area of today's Lafayette and Park streets, near where Barnard's malt house stood.

Connecticut's temperance movement dates back at least to the early 1800s. An undated letter from the Reverend N. Hewitt of Bridgeport, Conn., printed in an 1833 publication, "The Temperance Advocate," predicted that the temperance movement would "steadily advance amongst us" and that "temperance societies and revivals of religion are converting our young lawyers and barristers into ministers of the gospel."

Connecticut was among a dozen or so states that in the mid-1800s passed what were called Maine liquor laws, which sought to follow

Maine into a state of temperance. The movement that eventually resulted in the national Prohibition started in 1815 in Maine. Connecticut passed its own temperance law in 1834 with the encouragement of the Connecticut Temperance Society, which had incorporated in Hartford just five years earlier. Society agents advanced the cause by traveling around the state and holding rallies. In 1830 one agent, John Marsh, a Congregational minister, gave a speech in Pomfret to the Windham Temperance Society titled "Putnam and the Wolf, or The Monster Destroyed" that was reprinted and purchased by 150,000 hungry readers.[37]

Dr. Henry C. Beardslee of Monroe, Conn., was hired to travel throughout the state and visit the eight society auxiliaries to make sure that the cause of temperance was kept before the people.[38] The society included most of the boldfaced names at the time, including the Reverend Jeremiah Day, who would later serve as head of Yale College. (Day was plagued by a weak heart his entire life and asked in 1841 to be replaced as president of the society. Evidently the work of keeping spirits from the lips of Connecticut residents had worn him out.)

No less a figure than Horace Mann wrote that liquor laws were as important as the invention of printing.[39] "If temperance prevails," he wrote, "then Education can prevale [sic],—if Temperance fails, then

Horace Mann, c. 1900.
Photograph. Retrieved from
Library of Congress, www
.loc.gov/item/2002725457/

Education must fail."[40] He was coming at the issue from the view of a teacher who believed strongly that removing alcohol from the home would greatly benefit the children he sought to teach.

Hyperbole aside—well, no one could quite put hyperbole aside when it came to alcohol—the results of those stricter liquor laws in Connecticut, said one ecstatic observer, were nothing short of miraculous. Jails emptied. Families settled into comfortable homes. Women lovingly greeted their (formerly drunk) men back into the home and happily made their lunches to take to work. Traffic was safer. Children were happier.[41] Letters to the editor trumpeted the lack of drunks lounging in the streets of Frog Hollow and the rest of Hartford, and added that the "warmest friends to the law and its originators are the wives who were worse than widows, and the children who were worse than orphans, before its passage and enforcement."[42] Ministers rushed to give quotes to newspapers and made-up statistics to researchers, such as a diminution of crime by 75 percent, increased attendance in Sunday school, and anecdotes: "Little children that used to run and hide from their fathers when they came home drunk are now well dressed and run out to meet them."[43] It was all a bit breathless. Meanwhile, Connecticut's legislators, cleaving to the reality of their constituents' world, weakened the law bit by bit until it was eventually repealed in 1872.[44]

And so the hyperbole began again, from testimony at one public hearing in Hartford that with the increase in alcohol consumption crime had increased in Hartford by 400 percent. Even the secretary of state, Hiram Appleman, reported, "The whole number of persons committed to jail during the year is four thousand four hundred and eighty-one (4,481), being one thousand four hundred and ninety-six (1,496) more than in the preceding year." Hartford County reported a 115 percent increase of incarceration for drunkenness.[45] In 1887 temperance activists pushed for another prohibition and weren't satisfied when legislators could only summon the will to pass a resolution to submit a constitutional amendment to the voters. To bolster their argument, activists quoted statistics for the year ending June 1887: of the 6,849 crimes committed in the state, nearly half (49 percent) were for drunkenness.[46] In March 1915 a speech at the Hartford Get-Together Club by temperance activist A. A. Hopkins of New York was so popular that he made a return trip. Both men and women were invited to the second speech.

But over all, Connecticut loved liquor, and taverns remained the gathering places they'd been in colonial times. When the Eighteenth Amendment was put before the voters, Connecticut joined just one other state, Rhode Island, in refusing to ratify. Why? In his 2010 book "Last Call: The Rise and Fall of Prohibition," Daniel Okrent pointed to both states' heavy Catholic population (67 percent in Connecticut, and 76 percent in Rhode Island).[47] Then too both states had large immigrant populations whose members had settled in places like Frog Hollow, and immigrants as a group did not support Prohibition. In the words of the *New Haven Journal Courier,* "Connecticut is alone entitled to raise the flag of freedom in her hands and wave it aloft."[48] The state's more liberal stance on alcohol ran in stark contrast to Connecticut's earlier laws, according to temperance publications of the day, which touted the state's so-called blue laws—laws that prohibited commerce, and most other activities, on the Sabbath. "We see no likelihood of the return of such a law, although it is exceedingly probable that it will soon be a crime to sell a poison that makes a father go home on the Sabbath day and, instead of kissing his child, pitch it into the fireplace," said one.[49]

The *American Prohibition Year Book* from 1908 estimated that the average American spent $24.94 per year for alcohol, or $112.23 per family (assuming each family included 4.5 people), "which has been found approximately correct (varying slightly in different states)."[50] By 1920, after the passage of national Prohibition, the Hartford city health department credited the (relative) lack of alcohol to a decrease

Silver City men erect Barleycorn monument.
Connecticut Meriden, 1920. Photograph.
Retrieved from Library of Congress,
www.loc.gov/item/91796663/

in the death rate, particularly in suicides. In fact deaths by alcoholism averaged fourteen a year from 1914 to 1918, dropped to three in
1919, and city officials had counted just one death by alcoholism by
November 1920.[51] (The figures were compiled just fifteen months
after the institution of Prohibition, so the summation must be taken
with a grain of salt.)

For all the fervor of Prohibition supporters, no one could deny
the loss of revenue that accompanied a dry world. A December 1920
Hartford County Commissioners' report said the loss of revenues in
liquor licenses alone had put the county in the red by about $450,000,

or about $5.6 million in today's dollars. That was not the only financial loss from Prohibition. Add to it the loss of money once gleaned from residents jailed and fined for public drunkenness, and the financial loss to local government was significant.[52] In fact the lack of excise taxes on liquor sales revealed just how much local governments relied on the demon rum. Ken Burns, in his three-part 2011 PBS special on Prohibition, said New York alone lost 75 percent of its budget when liquor taxes dried up. The federal government, according to the special, lost eleven billion dollars in tax revenue, and spent three hundred million dollars to enforce the ban.[53]

A 1922 *Courant* story pronounced the national experiment—then two years old—a "failure." In fact, since Prohibition, the paper said, there'd been more arrests for public drunkenness, including arrests for driving while drunk, and more incidences of women drinking in public places.[54] Regardless, officials from the president on down wanted very much for the Noble Experiment to work, and police departments everywhere took enforcement seriously.

Enforcement by police created a different relationship with the public, one rooted in hostility. So-called respectable people who disagreed with Prohibition found themselves the target of the long arm of the law, and they didn't like it or appreciate it.[55] Some research shows that enforcement was applied selectively. Neighborhoods that were identified as problematic (either as home to too many newcomers—hello, Frog Hollow—or home to people who'd already run afoul of the law, or home to the poor—and hello, again and again) were the target of most law enforcement efforts.[56] Hartford police focused on Frog Hollow as a den of iniquity, and a haven for immigrants.

So to Frog Hollow came Isaac Kroopneck, husband of Sadie, a cop's cop who was assigned to the vice squad to enforce Prohibition. Kroopneck was part of a larger effort spearheaded by Hartford County state's attorney Hugh Alcorn, who was the son of Irish immigrants who'd grown up in Suffield in the northern part of the state. Alcorn's father had served in the Civil War and been captured—twice—as a prisoner of war. Alcorn senior came home from the war and battled alcoholism, which may have played into Alcorn's later aggressiveness around restricting alcohol. As a long-term state's attorney for Hartford County, Alcorn prosecuted more than fifteen thousand criminal cases, some of which resulted in national legislation around white slavery and medical standards. (He also prosecuted the murder cases that resulted in the play and movie *Arsenic and Old Lace*.)[57] In June 1923 Alcorn enlisted county detective Edward Hickey, his own appointee, and Hartford police Sergeant Isaac Kroopneck to lead a series of raids. He promised to shutter every saloon in the city and make Hartford "bone dry."

Kroopneck knew every liquor emporium in the city and he was single-minded in his pursuit of criminals. He once posed as a bartender at an establishment in the north end of Hartford, much to the disdain of lawyers prosecuting the case. One year, Kroopneck and others raided a farm just outside of town, discovered a fresh patch of earth, and dug deep enough to find a barrel of cheap liquor stored in pint and half-pint bottles.

Kroopneck and Hickey visited places with crowbars, axes, and chisels. The two raiders "instilled fear in the hearts of Hartford's bootleggers by their ruthless methods," according to a *Courant* article. That first summer 150 saloons were shut down, and it looked like Prohibition would be a success in the capital city.

But the early flush of success was fleeting. Revelers would watch as glass flew during a raid, and when Kroopneck and others left they'd simply sweep up the mess and start serving again. By April 1924 the *Courant* was reporting that "officials of the Hartford police department are becoming cynical when discussing the Volstead Act and persistently maintain there is more drunkenness now than before prohibition went into effect."

A *Courant* story from November 1921 reported that Frog Hollow's best-known bootlegging establishment was the House of Three Knocks at 54 Lawrence. People who intended to enter the establishment had to knock three times and then say "cuckoo." Run by Josephine Valenski, the place was raided repeatedly by police, and Valenski was arrested multiple times. On one occasion, according to the *Courant*, a Sergeant Sutherland knocked three times, said "cuckoo," and then tried to push his way into the door, which was held by four chains. He and others broke in the door, forced the occupants to dump the contents of a pitcher into a sink, and were then joined by Kroopneck, who came with a wrench, removed a trap from beneath the sink, and poured the fluid into a bottle for evidence. Prior to the raid, Kroopneck had sat out in front of the house for four days, waiting for the right moment.

On another occasion, Kroopneck crashed through the front door at 12 Lawrence Street, the home of Ignatz and Mary Gozorowski. There too the door was held by chains, but Kroopneck was not deterred. In 1918 Hartford's Court of Common Council awarded him $366.09 to reimburse him for expenses incurred while he defended himself in a suit for wrongful death.[58] Earlier, Kroopneck was sued for ten thousand dollars by Nicholas Kozy, brother of Michael Kozy, who'd been killed in an assault by Kroopneck in the performance of his job. The council found that although Kozy had died, Kroopneck had performed his duties properly.

Alcorn held office for more than three decades and led prosecutions through Prohibition, but he far overestimated his ability to ferret out speakeasy wrongdoers. By the time Prohibition was repealed in 1933, Connecticut was long done with being dry. During a 1932 referendum, nearly 86 percent of Connecticut residents—more than in any other state—said they were ready for a drink.[59]

Finding a pastime in a working-class neighborhood involved navigating the Puritan need for industry (personal industry, as in the work ethic) and the very real need of taking a break. With increased industrialization came a desire for relaxation, and it came in the form of a leather ball and wooden bat. Hartford's first professional baseball team was the Hartford Dark Blues, who played at a diamond built in Colt Park in the south part of the city in 1874.[60] The team only lasted a couple of years, but it gave the national pastime an early foothold in the capital city. The city's love of the game grew exponentially.

In 1904 Gus Fischer, owner of a dry goods shop on Asylum Street, organized a factory baseball league meant strictly for shop teams. Fischer was a character. In addition to sinking significant money into the league, he kept a trained dog that, according to news reports at the time, could juggle a crust of bread and a coin. Most of the games were scheduled around the city in public parks, and the competition was followed closely by the city sports writers. "There is plenty of good material in some of the shops, and some first-rate games may be looked for," said the *Courant* in 1904.[61] The season started in June of that year, and on one Sunday afternoon five games were played, back-to-back, to sellout crowds who gathered with blankets and baskets to watch the marathon. The games drew such attention and ignited such passions that by the next year the league had to appoint a board of directors to "settle all disputes."[62] Within a few seasons, bleachers were built in parks around the city. Picnics and dances were held in conjunction with the games. The *Courant* awarded nicknames to the popular players and breathlessly guessed the outcome of each game. Beyond bragging rights, the league champion team would take home a silver cup, provided by Gus Fischer.

Meanwhile, clergy argued over the morality of playing baseball on the Lord's Day, but a Sunday *Courant* editorial on August 10, 1901, said, "There is no use in trying not to see the fact that a new Sunday has come, and that the man who works for six days is going to have refreshment and recreation on the seventh." The man, more often than not, worked at one of the powerhouse factories and played for a factory team. Baseball teams representing Billings & Spencer, and

Industrial Baseball League, Hartford, Conn. Miriam and Ira D. Wallach
Division of Art, Prints and Photographs: Photography Collection, New York
Public Library Digital Collections, http://digitalcollections.nypl.org/items
/510d47d9-bb2e-a3d9-e040-e00a18064a99

Pope, enjoyed a hearty rivalry on the diamond, as did the Hollow's
Pratt & Whitney and Capewell Horse Nail, to the north.

Fun was one thing, boisterousness was something else again. In
a Sunday sermon in August 1901, the Reverend J. T. Winters at the
Church of the Immaculate Conception encouraged parents to exercise supervision over their overactive children. From the *Courant*:
"Young people as a whole, he thought, were too prone to late-at-night
promenades, and young fellows were too apt to congregate upon
corners, carrying on conversation in a loud tone and in other ways
disturbing the rest of those who desired repose and whose wishes
were entitled to respect."[63]

He also bemoaned the behavior of younger children who, as well,
romped and created a disturbance at an hour when quiet was pref-

erable (though what that hour was is not recorded). In a sermon delivered a few days later, the Reverend Winters rained down condemnation on Sunday baseball. Baseball, like those romping children, was too loud. It also took up too much time. But the good reverend was willing to compromise. If a full baseball game wasn't to be had on Sundays, a "knock-up" or "catch-out" might be acceptable. Workingmen, after all, were entitled to their harmless recreation, so long as they weren't boisterous or disruptive of other people's devotions. He suggested that people could play a light game at home, on their streets, but that the games that drew hundreds to the parks (and away from the pews) should be left to the actual players, and that families should stay away from the spectacle. This he assumed would have the desired effect of shutting things down, because what baseball player would participate in the sport without spectators?[64]

A priest was powerful in Frog Hollow but the pull of baseball was stronger, and a couple of weeks later five hundred people gathered at Pope Park, with another two hundred fifty on a nearby slope, to watch Sunday baseball—the boisterous kind, with cheering and betting. A heavy police presence frightened the players into submission, though the police had decided to let the players go three innings before they broke up the game.

Meanwhile, that same week, a man known as the Mayor of Frog Hollow, Wilson Street resident John F. Gunshanan, manager of the Workingmen's Club and a former baseball player, went to city hall to try to convince the real mayor, Alexander Harbison, that Pope Park neighbors actually preferred the games to go on. He included a list of neighbors who supported baseball, particularly those on Hamilton Street, next to the park. At the time of Gunshanan's visit, Harbison was in Torrington at a celebration for firefighters, so Gunshanan, who disavowed having any real political ambitions, left a statement that insisted the game was played under strict rules prohibiting profanity, quarreling, card playing, and "drinking from a bottle." He closed with a quote from a *Courant* editorial that "a new Sunday has come, and that the man who works for six days is going to have refreshment and recreation on the seventh."[65]

The issue of Sunday baseball remained unresolved in 1906 when Gunshanan organized a charity baseball game (that included no less an emissary than Connie Mack of the Philadelphias) to raise money for a bed for consumptives at a local hospital. Rather quickly, a law was passed banning Sunday baseball, and so Gunshanan called it off. He had intended to raise three thousand dollars for the hospital but resigned himself to organizing a game on a weekday, between professional players, after the regular baseball season. In 1908 he was able to secure lodging and food for the visiting Red Sox and Philadelphia Athletics, though they played in New Britain and Meriden, not Hartford.[66]

Given the potential for healthy rosters among factory workers, Frog Hollow became the sports mecca for Hartford. The neighborhood also had a football team, the Tiger Cadets, which began advertising for opponents in 1909—"The Cadets would like to play any team in the state at 130 pounds"—and gave a Ward Street address for any interested opponents.[67] Players were expected to attend practices, and those who missed were dropped from the team and, adding to the shame, their names were published in the *Courant*. The team was still advertising for opponents in 1911, but a shortage of opponents could not be taken for a lack of passion. Jack Dwyer, of Manchester, wrote a letter in 1912 to the *Courant* "sporting" editor: "In this morning's Courant on your sporting page there was an article describing the Carlisle–Frog Hollow Tiger game in this place on Sunday. The writer of that article is either near-sighted or his knowledge of football must be dated back to the time that Noah landed the ark. The average weight of the Carlisle team, with the heaviest men in the line, is 147 pounds. The Tiger team is without a doubt a very good one, but, believe me, their backfield never for a minute startled anybody out there."[68]

Nevertheless, the Tigers made it to the city championship, where they lost to the Major Athletic Club in a driving snowstorm before a large crowd. They were, said the *Courant*, simply outgunned. (Not to worry: the Tigers won the 1915 championship, 13–0.) The Tigers merged with their rival, the Ramblers, in 1920 to create a football powerhouse.

In November 1920 supporters held a dinner to honor neighborhood notables at Immaculate Conception's school hall. Included among the evening's honorees was new Trinity College president Remsen Brinckerhoff Ogilby, who had just begun the job. The Reverend Ogilby was a Harvard graduate, an army chaplain during the War to End All Wars, and he'd started a school for boys in the Philippines. He had hoped to be sent overseas, but the armistice was signed while he was still awaiting orders.[69] Ogilby had an impressive resume, and on that November night he was welcomed warmly; but the biggest hand of the night (and a purse full of money from the team supporters) went to Ramblers-Tiger captain Harold Herbert "Spud" Drew. When Drew stood to thank the crowd, he became too overcome to speak and sat down without saying anything.[70] He was later named captain to the *Courant's* All-City Eleven. Eventually, a neighborhood basketball team took up when the football season ended, with every bit as much fan fervor as greeted the Rambler-Tigers.

Sports in the neighborhood were a great distraction from the challenges of living in Frog Hollow. In the winter of 1918, reported a *Courant* article, families had taken to saving coal by huddling around their wood-fired kitchen stoves—new additions to homes that were "coming into their own." Even if residents and businesses had coal in their cellar, they tended not to use it for fear of public censure. Police officers inspecting cellars discovered mountains of unused coal, and not just in the homes of poorer families. "In the home of one woman whose name is prominently connected with movements to benefit the poor, about one-half a ton of coal was found, although she has a big house. The Hotel Regal showed one-eighth of a ton, and the building next to it had eighteen tons." To preserve coal "during a brutally cold winter," the federal government instituted so-called Garfield Holidays, named after a government official responsible for fuel supplies, that required industry closures for five days in January 1918, as well as "cold Mondays," where on every Monday through late March of that year, offices and stores east of the Mississippi—where the vast bulk of the country's population lived—could not be heated with fuel. The closures and bans had little effect on shortages, though.[71]

Later that year the Connecticut State Council of Defense shared with Thomas W. Russell, the U.S. fuel administrator for the state, a list of ways to keep coal use to a minimum, in a flyer that was meant to be tacked up near furnaces and kitchen ranges. Frog Hollow residents were instructed to "use brains as well as coal" by starting furnaces later in the day, and they were encouraged to keep houses at a temperate 68 degrees.[72] Wood often took the place of coal, but given the increased demand, the price pushed even that fuel out of reach of some families.[73]

Wars demand sacrifices, as does peace. As World War I ended and defense work slowed, Hartford manufacturers began to fire women who weren't supporting families, and they gave first preference to soldiers returning from the war. Wars "changed the boundaries of many nations, transformed economies, disrupted political systems, and severely strained social life," but after the guns were silenced a binary work world divided between male and female slipped back into place.[74] With the end of World War I, the war economy shifted and many of the people who'd been employed—and not just women—were, according to the *Courant*, added to the "army of the unemployed."[75] The relative egalitarian nature of the wartime Hartford workforce reverted back to men-only. President Herbert Hoover's Section 213 of the 1932 National Economy Act prohibited more than one family member from working in a civil service job. Private companies followed suit, including the New England Telephone and Telegraph Co., and others fired their female employees in 1931. A survey by the National Industrial Conference Board said that "84 percent of insurance companies, 65 percent of banks, and 63 percent of public utilities restricted the hiring of married women," though such a policy did little to create more jobs for unemployed men.[76]

While women were losing jobs, white powerbrokers were squeezing African Americans out of Frog Hollow and the city's south end in a series of moves that were both illegal and effective. In addition to redlining were higher taxes, random demands of proof of home ownership, and threatened foreclosures, which worked to intimidate and herd many of Hartford's African American residents into the north end.[77] By 1920 the foundation had been laid for creating in the north end a uniquely black city within the city, with segregated schools, churches, and businesses.

And still African Americans moved to Connecticut. The southern economy stagnated between the wars, and out-migration ran at about 7 percent.[78] But letters sent back home from Frog Hollow let people know that a boom was going on in the North and a person had to be crazy not to come take advantage of it.

The new residents were responding as well to efforts of organizations such as the National League on Urban Conditions, which actively recruited southern workers for the state's tobacco fields. Young black men in particular responded in droves. Southern white political leaders were mostly silent on the vigilante violence that was a constant in the lives of black residents. Recruits from areas such as southwest Georgia were escaping frequent lynchings for a land that while equally segregated, had less violent methods of containment. They were coming to a land where law enforcement jobs tended to go to the Irish and sanitation jobs to the Italian, but perhaps there was room for them in the fields or the scattered factories.[79] Hundreds of thousands of black families decided to chance it.

Most of these recruits were young men, and in the summer of 1944 they included one Martin Luther King Jr. At age fifteen this was the future civil rights leader's first trip outside of the South, and he wrote to his father that June: "On our way here, we saw some things I had never anticipated to see. After we passed Washington there was no discrimination at all and the white people here are very nice. We go to any place we want to and sit any where we want to."[80] The trip back south meant a switch to a segregated car in Washington, and King recorded that on moving to the back of the train he felt a curtain had "dropped on my selfhood."[81] King's observations reveal just how segregated must have been his native Atlanta, for even if the white people in Connecticut were nice, he as a black teenager would not have enjoyed the same benefits and opportunities as a white teenager, even in multiethnic, multiracial Hartford.

At the time of King's labor in the fields, the Reverend Robert Andrew Moody, a New Jersey native, was actively pushing for integration in Hartford and in the fire and police departments. In 1948 Moody wrote about Connecticut segregation in a six-part series in the *Courant* titled "A Negro Views the North": "Here in New England no legislative fiat has kept the Negro at the bottom. Instead the same result has been achieved through a 'gentleman's agreement.'"

Connecticut was hardly Beulah Land. While African American residents were moving north, the factory jobs that attracted them were often moving south. By the 1920s, Connecticut was already seeing its industry move to the more manufacturer-friendly South with its lack of protections for workers.[82] In fact, during the 1920s fourteen of the state's forty-seven textile mills moved south.[83]

During World War II, as had happened in the Great War, women were called from their homes to work in jobs formerly held by men now serving on the battlefront. Twelve million men went into the military, while the wheels of industry needed eighteen million new workers.[84] Women were encouraged to enter the workforce by a massive effort from the federal Office of War Information, which was established in 1942 to consolidate information efforts of already-existing agencies such as the Office of Government Reports, and to distribute propaganda—there is no other word for it—at home and abroad. Abroad, that might mean handing out pin cushions with Hitler's face on them. At home, that meant once again convincing the female half of the population that they could best serve their countries by entering the factories and manufacturing companies formerly considered strictly men's work.

This was accomplished in a variety of ways, some subtle, some not. The U.S. Office of War Information's Book and Magazine Bureau was responsible for ensuring that printed material reflected the best war efforts of the United States. A woman living in Frog Hollow could walk to Park Street and purchase a magazine such as *True Story*, which formerly might have been full of stories about sexual infidelity or family conflicts but during the war effort switched to more practical fare, such as how to deal with a husband who didn't want his wife to enter the labor force. The Office of War Information had identified reluctant husbands as the main reason women weren't leaving the home for jobs. A November 1943 letter from a factory worker lamented that she had started work in a defense plant and was making more money than her husband, and he wanted her to quit and come back home. The response from another reader was that the woman's defense job was temporary and that the husband should put country before his own comfort. And besides, the reader had cajoled, "Do you think for one moment that she will be a machinist for the remainder of her natural life? You know how feminine she is, don't you?"[85] (In fact, between the end of the war and 1946, two million women returned home.[86]) Throughout media—books, magazines, and movies—the message was that children and husband at home would be fine; older children could pitch in, and husbands too, in order for America to win the war. Victory and happy homes did not need to be mutually exclusive. Signs in shops along Park Street reminded women that their efforts were important to the war effort: "What Job Is Mine on the Victory Line?"[87] "Save Your Cans. Help Pass the Ammunition."[88]

The message landed. In five years of World War II, "the female labor force grew by more than 50 percent from 11.9 million in 1940 to a wartime peak of 19.1 million. The proportion of all women who were employed increased from 27.6 percent to 37 percent according to government statistics."[89] In 1943, 4.5 million women worked in manufacturing industries nationwide, or 30 percent of all wage earners. Most of the women hired had no previous factory experience, according to the Women's Bureau of the U.S. Department of Labor, yet they were considered "well suited to many kinds of industrial work" and were considered "superior to men at certain tasks, particularly those which require dexterity and attention to details."[90]

Historically, the textile and apparels industries have been women's entry point into the job market, but the war opened metal, industrial chemicals, and rubber industries, which were particularly aggressive in recruiting women. Until the early 1940s, factories still mostly hired men, and any women who were brought on generally worked lower-paying jobs. Until the war, most better-paying work offered to women was strictly seasonal. As the war expanded, the male workforce depleted and factory owners along Rifle Lane/Capitol Avenue hired women. In Frog Hollow and elsewhere, the war eroded so-called marriage bars, policies that had precluded companies from hiring married women, which had been in place since the 1930s.

Manufacturing jobs in Frog Hollow paid better than domestic work formerly done by women. The jobs were more stable and they offered more benefits. Consequently, between 1920 and 1950, the percentage of women working in domestic services slipped from 39 to 5 percent. The percentage of women working in "manufacturing, machine shops, small arms manufacturing" and similar pursuits held steady at 20 to 25 percent. Meanwhile, the percentage of female work-force in the fields of teaching and nursing—professional work—rose from 9 to 15 percent. During that same period, the growing insurance industry attracted a high of 39 percent of the female workforce.[91]

With the exodus from home into the workforce, families needed support, which meant that policies toward the care of children had to change. Not every Frog Hollow family had older relatives who could step in to take care of children while their parents worked, who could prepare meals and otherwise keep a house running. The federal government mostly failed to provide support. Part of the reluctance of the government to step in was that the traditional role of women in the private sphere was considered off-limits to public policies. The few public efforts by the government to help mothers entering the workforce were "haphazard, minimal and ambivalent"—when action was taken at all.[92] Into the breach stepped employers, who began to change their way of doing things, from adding daycare centers on-site to commissioning childcare providers who lived within walking dis-tance of the factories.

Women joined the workforce outside the home for a variety of rea-sons, including their need for money, their sense of patriotic duty, and their desire to escape boredom.[93] Electric Boat in Groton, recruited navy wives whose husbands were away at war.[94] Unlike World War I's shifting workforce, the increase in women during the 1940s was more than just a blip. The greatest increase of women in the Amer-ican workforce occurred after 1940—with a 34 percent increase just between 1940 and 1960.[95] Prior to 1940, participation in the labor force was a venue for younger women. These were mostly unmarried women, or if they were married, they hadn't yet had children.[96]

The need for more war industry workers in Hartford opened doors for many, including employees of color, who quickly set down roots. That had to happen, or else the job would be left to nonprofit orga-nizations with far fewer resources.

5. *To Be Recognized*

THE CHILDREN OF FROG HOLLOW FIND
CHAMPIONS, AND THE NEWSIES FIGHT BACK

Anayaliz Rivera, age ten, and Kyla Picart, age eleven, can barely contain themselves. They and twelve or so other fourth-graders at the after-school program at Mi Casa Family Services and Educational Center on Park Street, a part of Hispanic Health Council, are planning a party. But this is not just any party. The children are planning a Mother's Day dinner for the mothers who are homeless in their Frog Hollow neighborhood. There will be flowers and balloons and a raffle basket and as much food as they can gather from their parents, who will cook and seek donations from neighborhood organizations.

The girls organize meetings. They make them mandatory for their parents by guilting them into coming. It doesn't take much. These parents are involved already, but the kids tell them, "This is our project and we are your children and you should support us," and so the parents sign on.

The children are keenly aware that homelessness exists in their community. A few summers ago, as part of Transformando el Futuro (Transforming the Future), the children created a booklet, "The Footsteps of a Homeless Person." They interviewed people who are homeless and took pictures of the authors and the subjects, and they educated themselves about homelessness. One poetic page in the book includes this: "Someone can have the world at their fingertips one day and have nothing the next day. Like the flip of a switch." The children also wrote about the lack of affordable housing in their city. They suggested that abandoned buildings could be rehabilitated as homes with bedrooms and kitchens. So this party is informed by a deep understanding of what it means to be homeless in Frog Hollow.

"We wanted to do something nice," said Anayaliz, pushing her glasses up her nose. "We wanted to be generous."

Kyla expected ten mothers. Anayaliz quickly amended that to thirty.

But it rains the day of the dinner, and just five mothers show up. Still, that is five mothers from South Park Inn over on Main Street who receive a pink carnation, a warm welcome, and a show of Puerto Rican folk dance, complete with Anayaliz and Kyla and others in beautiful skirts. The girls throw themselves into the routine while parents and others stand just on the periphery, phones hoisted to take videos and photos. The finale involves Anayaliz being hoisted into the air by two boys who are in their class. "You're lucky I didn't drop you," one of them says to her, once they lowered her to the floor.

This kind of event is precisely what Jorge L. Rivera had in mind when he founded Mi Casa. Rivera came to Hartford in the late 1980s. He'd been an attorney on the island and moved to the mainland to improve his English. He thought that he'd study for the bar, but his community needed him more than he needed to practice law. He started to work with young people who'd been through the court system, and a few years later he decided to work on keeping youths out of the court system in the first place.

Mi Casa Family Services and Educational Center is part of the Hispanic Health Council and offers a variety of student and parent programs meant to encourage families to focus on education. Through its homework and tutoring programs, Mi Casa has helped

Anayaliz Rivera (left), ten, and Kyra Picart, eleven,
perform a Puerto Rican folk dance for homeless
mothers in Frog Hollow at a dinner the children
planned at the Mi Casa Campus of Hispanic
Health Council. May 2017. Author photo

cut down on chronic absence and helped mold Maria Sánchez Ele-
mentary into a strong community school.

Yet this program and others have long faced significant budget cuts,
which were even more pronounced when the government debated
ending community development block grants. How do you plan for
the future when you don't know the financial hit you're about to
take? What do you tell children already enrolled in your program?
And where do those children and the children not yet old enough to
enroll go after school? They go to the streets, where, as Rivera said,
they may not learn the kind of community engagement sponsored by
Mi Casa. It's the kind of thing that can keep you up at night; Rivera
muses about the uncertainty as the children chatter, the mothers fill
their plates, and everyone settles in for a nice meal.

As the room grows quiet, one of the guests looks at her heaping plate and says, "I think I may cry."

Frog Hollow has always been about faith—faith in a God, and faith in a better life. From the middle of the last century, that faith fueled a unique brand of community activism that was one part Saul Alinsky, and one part liberation theology taught by generations of Catholic priests before the theology was labeled as such. Take, for example, Sacred Heart (Sagrado Corazón) Church. Sacred Heart Church was organized by German immigrants in the 1870s in the basement of another church on Hartford's South Green. In 1917 the congregation moved to their new building on Eli and Winthrop, and rather quickly the congregation became the touchstone for a succession of immigrants, including Italians and Irish. By the mid-1950s, a new generation of Puerto Ricans (including mover and shaker Maria Sánchez) had moved into Frog Hollow, so that the church just north of their neighborhood became the epicenter of political activism. Advocates opened San Juan Center in the basement, where teachers offered Head Start and other social service programs. A tutorial center taught a generation of Puerto Rican students, such as Carmen Cotto, that they could succeed. Cotto remembers Brother Marcus Turcotte testing her—as the Hartford school system hadn't done—and finding that she had made it to her sophomore year with dyslexia. Once Brother Marcus taught her about her unique way of learning, Cotto said, she was able to finish high school and go on to college.

"Hartford schools never tested me," Cotto said. "It was the church that tested me."[1]

Hartford has long been a battlefield for childhood—what it is, how much it should be protected, and who should protect it—and as such, Hartford's educational opportunities have always been multi-tiered. For children from families with resources, education has been a given. For the rest, not so much, and so it has been from the beginning.

In 1829 a Sunday school for Hartford's Roman Catholic children opened in the office of the newspaper the *Catholic Press*. On the one hand, the school was proof that the religious landscape was changing in Hartford and Frog Hollow. On the other, a separate school system wasn't so much the desire of the Roman Catholics to separate as a marker for the earlier (Protestant) settlers' disdain for the Catholic Church.

That same year, as more Roman Catholics moved to Hartford, the Reverend Bernard O'Cavanagh came to town to administer fulltime to a flock that was growing too quickly for an itinerant priest. For a time, the Reverend O'Cavanagh lived in a hotel. The hotel was much to his liking. Hartford, however, was not. The place was too provincial, and O'Cavanagh was not interested in leading a starter church in what can only be described as hostile land.

Most of the worshipers in the growing Frog Hollow neighborhood belonged either to the Congregational, Episcopal, or Baptist churches. Ironically, Puritans who had come seeking religious freedom were quick to make it difficult for non-Puritans (particularly Catholics) to worship as they saw fit. In fact Connecticut had a reputation for being particularly intolerant toward Catholicism. An early history of the Catholic Church in Connecticut said that the "spirit of antagonism to all things Catholic was everywhere. Children imbibed it at the maternal breast. It pervaded the religious literature of the times and inspired the philippics of the clergy."[2] The reference to fiery and angry speeches decrying Catholicism was not hyperbole, and it explains why, at a time when most schools were church sponsored, Roman Catholics preferred to educate their children themselves and keep them as far as possible from Protestant schools.

Before a Catholic church was established in Hartford, priests offered Mass in private houses, printing offices, public halls, and sometimes in barns that were, according to a history of the Hartford archdiocese, "suitably prepared for the joyous occasion. . . . But what mattered it? Was not the divine Victim of the sacrifice born in a lowly stable, and were not the dumb beasts among the first witnesses of His advent?"[3]

To house the growing flock, O'Cavanagh's bishop, Benedict J. Fenwick, found an abandoned Episcopal church whose members had moved to a new building. A story circulated that when the Episcopal priest was with the Catholic bishop looking over the building, the priest remarked, with some pride, that his congregation had a new building and no longer needed the old one. The bishop is said to have retorted, "Yes, and you have a fine new religion, and we will keep the old one."[4]

In 1830 Catholic residents in Hartford established their first church—the Church of the Most Holy Trinity—at the corner of Main and Talcott streets. The building included an organ and a full basement for their Sunday school. In those first few weeks the church was filled mostly with Protestants anxious to see what Catholics did on Sundays, and the congregation's song leader was a thirteen-year-old organist, who was paid ninety dollars a year for her services. (By comparison, an adult shoemaker could make roughly three times that in a year, and a pair of boots ran about $4.50.)[5]

That same year, a day school for Catholic children was opened in the church basement, but just as the Catholic faithful were building a home, the Reverend O'Cavanagh began to petition to be moved. That request was granted, though fifty-four members of his flock signed a petition asking that he be forced to stay. They even threatened to withdraw financial support from his successor.[6] Why the flock wanted to keep a reluctant priest is lost to history, and their efforts came to naught anyway. O'Cavanagh went to Detroit, and after a rocky start his successor, the Reverend James Fitton, established himself and was eventually credited with alleviating some diocese debt in the few years he was in Hartford.

By 1850 the capital city had a population of 13,555 souls with growing needs. Unlike today, in the beginning Sunday schools were not places to park children while the adults worshipped separately. Instead, Sunday schools were charitable and missionary enterprises where the Gospel came wrapped in cornbread and boiled eggs. The schools administered food and clothing, as well as Bible lessons— though the emphasis was on the former.

As the population grew, similar schools began to pop up around the capital city. Between 1850 and 1858, ten new schools were established to provide relief to the city's poor. In 1859 the schools' work was incorporated within the Hartford City Missionary Society, led by a man named David Hawley, who became known as "Father."[7] Father Hawley was a favorite charity for Hartford luminaries like Mark Twain, and he served in the capacity of benevolent leader for decades.[8]

But even a benevolent leader couldn't protect workers from the industrial machine. While technology pushed the city into the future, more of Frog Hollow's newest residents arrived without the necessary skills. It was the nineteenth century's version of today's challenge of the unskilled laborer. Frog Hollow residents weren't competing with artificial intelligence or robots but with steam-powered machines that called for a more literate workforce.

In 1855 Connecticut legislators, seeking to protect workers, passed a law that limited workdays to ten hours, but the law carried a provision that if employer and employee agreed to longer days, then longer days were allowed. Since there was no oversight as to what "agreed" meant, the law was considered mostly for show and mostly ineffectual.[9] That same year, Connecticut legislators passed a law that banned children age nine and younger from working in factories. In response to a push by teachers and other social activists, the age was increased to ten the following year.[10] Compared to surrounding states, Connecticut had a reputation for treating childhood as a unique and important moment in life, and the state also passed, ahead of neighboring Massachusetts, a law that limited the labor of children under fourteen years to ten hours a day.[11] Childhood—and by inference children—had gained in importance during colonial times, partly because of the potential for a labor force but also as a metaphor for the new nation itself.[12]

The importance of protecting childhood was balanced against the need for employees, and the protection of children often came up wanting. As far back as 1813, children who worked in factories were required by Connecticut law to receive lessons in reading, writing, and arithmetic.[13] Employers were also required to see to the morals of their young employees. To enforce the rules, leaders in each town were required to create a board whose members performed annual checks. Board members were required to report infractions to the county.[14] Even with the boards and the checking, this too was a fairly toothless law. There wasn't much stomach for actually turning in offenders and perhaps cutting into a company's profits. Child labor in Connecticut continued mostly unabated into the next century, until an activist photographer and a concerned librarian teamed up to show how damaging it could be. More on that in a moment.

In 1890, 1.5 million children between the ages of ten and fourteen were "gainfully employed," according to the U.S. Census Bureau.[15] From 1870 to 1900, children who were working in industrial jobs (think textile mills in Massachusetts, or tool-and-die manufacturers in Frog Hollow) increased threefold, from 350,000 to 1.1 million.[16] Working in a factory was one thing. The children were out of sight and so only the most dedicated reformers took notice. When children worked the streets as shiners (shoe-shiners) or newsies (newspaper deliverers), the public began to question the wisdom of children with jobs.

Restricting the size of the labor force was a hard sell to industrialists and others, who balked against losing employees who worked for peanuts and who didn't question eleven- and twelve-hour days. Consequently, despite its reputation for protecting childhood in theory, Connecticut was slow to adopt child labor reform. For decades, only the thinnest of protections existed for "factory children," the state's most vulnerable "employees." Fortunately, in Hartford the children had on their side a do-gooder librarian and a handful of fierce matrons who wanted more from, and for, their state. The tide would turn in a spectacular way on the thin backs of resolute newsies.

Just after the turn of the last century, the life of Hartford newsies was captured by photographer Lewis Wickes Hine. Hine used his camera to illustrate injustices, particularly among children who were drawn into the industrial machine. Hine, a Wisconsin native, shot a series of photos at Ellis Island beginning in 1904 to show immigrants teeming to American shores. He was hired by the National Child Labor Committee in 1908, and he traveled twelve thousand miles in one year, sometimes posing as a fire inspector to gain access to child laborers.[17] His photos spoke volumes during the committee's lobbying efforts.

In 1909 Hine turned his camera on to the plight of Hartford's two-hundred-some newsies, some as young as six years old, who took to streets and bars (drunks were good customers, one newsboy told Hine) to earn a living.[18] Ironically, Hine himself had dropped out of school at age fifteen and worked a series of jobs until a Wisconsin teacher took an interest in him.[19] The same teacher encouraged him to take photos of immigrants coming in to Ellis Island. Hine, who continued his work through 1924, was an early reformer who believed children are endowed with certain rights—including the right to be children.[20]

Connecticut was slow to pass child labor reform legislation, including compulsory school attendance laws; one of the biggest opponents of child labor in the Nutmeg State were the labor unions.[21] A 1905 report said, "Connecticut feels apparently no urgent need of improvement in its old established law. Its industries are chiefly of a character which enable men to support their families, and do not call for the work of children."

In stepped a steely librarian who refused to believe that a childhood should be spent peddling. In 1901 Caroline M. Hewins, one of Hartford's early child librarians, helped incorporate the Hartford Social Settlement Association, with a specific interest in the children who worked in the factories and on the streets of the capital city. Hewins was the daughter of a successful haberdasher. She was reading by age four and moved to Hartford in 1875 to be the librarian at the Young Men's Institute, a private subscription library with six hundred members who paid three dollars a year to have access to the collection's twenty thousand books. There she made it her business to expunge inappropriate children's books in favor of the "immortal four," which for her included Optic, Alger, Castlemon, and Martha Finley.[22] Hewins lived in the settlement house at 15 North Street for twelve years, and in 1903 no less a social activism luminary than Jane Addams came to speak at the organization's annual meeting.

Newsies have been romanticized in movies and plays, but the work was dirty and dangerous and the hours were long for very little money. Still, the pittance brought in by children as young as

Caroline M. Hewins. Courtesy of Hartford History Center, Hartford Public Library

Girls coming through the alley. The smallest girl has been selling for two years. Lewis Wickes Hines, photographer. Location: Hartford, Connecticut. Library of Congress Prints and Photographs Division, Washington, D.C. 20540, http://hdl.loc.gov/loc.pnp/pp.print

six helped families put food on the table. Those news routes were feeding younger siblings, older grandparents, and sometimes, when parents were unable to find work, the entire family.

In 1898 the *Bridgeport Daily Herald* carried a long piece about a newsie uprising over a raise in the price of newspapers. The newsies struck and even marched through Hartford with signs like "Dose Who Buys De World and Journal Ain't Friends to Hartford Newsboys" (from the Bridgeport paper). The strike ended within the week when the New York papers dropped back to the original price. Said the Bridgeport paper, "That ended the strike and the unintelligible jargon of the newsboy once more disturbs the peaceful air in Hartford."[23]

After a three-hour meeting in May 1909, the newsboys and newsgirls formed the Hartford Newsboys' Association, with the stated mission of fighting back when newspaper titans in far-off New York started refusing to buy back unsold copies of their newspapers from news agents. They were helped in the meeting by the Hartford settlement's head social worker, Mary Graham Jones, and the head of the local cigar makers' union; the latter first came to observe but ended up giving the children advice on how to organize. The children elected officers: Harry Brightman, Mooris (that's how the name was spelled in the newspaper) Zalkavitz, Michael Levy, and Nathan Feldstein, the latter of whom had been arrested after a misunderstanding between himself and two young boys who'd stolen his horse and carriage. As their New York colleagues had done in 1899, the boys and girls of Hartford refused to sell New York papers, and the local businesses supported them. Even Herman P. Kopplemann, who'd been selling the boys the New York papers and who'd discouraged them from striking, supported them, to the point that he paid Feldstein's bail to get him out of custody.[24]

The newsies were lucky to have advocates and organizations in place meant to protect them. John F. Gunshanan, for one, was Frog Hollow through and through. He had graduated from Hartford High in 1904, a year after his brother James. The men would eventually live across the street from one another on Affleck Street, hard by the neighborhood's Zion Hill Cemetery. Gunshanan loved sports and in 1918 was appointed to a committee to raise funds for athletic equipment for Hartford youth.[25] Gunshanan had his finger in every pie, and not just in the neighborhood. In 1909 he had begun a four-year appointment on another committee to establish county homes for people with tuberculosis.[26] He served on a committee to study houses of comfort, or public restrooms.[27]

But it was Frog Hollow's children who interested Gunshanan most. As residents started to notice more children playing on the streets of Frog Hollow—particularly Park Street, where traffic was heavy and children could get hurt—calls went out for a vacation school to open at Lawrence Street School. Gunshanan immediately jumped on board.

Vacation schools were part of the nationwide progressive movement that provided summer school to children who were growing up impoverished on dirty, crowded streets. In Chicago the schools were "one of the most beneficent and wisely conducted charities of the city," according to Dr. E. Benjamin Andrews, the city's superintendent in 1899.[28] The curriculum contained some class work, but students in vacation school mostly spent time on lessons that appealed to their creative sides. After all, according to a 1909 report from the Connecticut State Board of Education, "interest in education is not limited to the actual work in the schoolroom. Many look with eager expectancy to the extension of public education" such as that offered in night schools and vacation schools.[29] The first discussions of vacation schools for Hartford started in the winter of 1897 with speeches given by proponents to civic organizations. When classes opened at Brown School, far more children applied than there was room for, so families were restricted to sending one child. The understanding was that the child lucky enough to attend summer school would then go home and share what he or she had learned during the day.

The children began the day singing a hymn and then all the verses of "America," which inspired a *Courant* writer to opine that the children reciting the Pledge of Allegiance "suddenly transformed the smallest bit of humanity in to a potential citizen with all his responsibilities."[30] Vacation schools offered an extraordinary opportunity for children in the hollow, but the idea was not universally embraced. When the schools were on the agenda at one Hartford meeting, neighbors argued back and forth about the potential dangers, such as infection. The city's board of health had recommended that all city schools be closed to prevent the spread of diseases such as smallpox—which had struck another city school that year—and scarlet fever, always a concern, during the warmer months.

But Gunshanan argued that education should continue through the summer—educated children made better workers, after all—and the schools should include a gym for the workers who came to Frog Hollow for their jobs. Despite arguments from opponents that Frog Hollow should not provide recreation for workers who might not live in the neighborhood, Gunshanan made some persuasive arguments and the motion eventually passed. A vacation school was opened at the Lawrence Street school in the summer of 1903, and yes, it included a gym.[31]

Still, for many of Frog Hollow's children, the opportunity for a summer vacation school was only a dream. In order for the children to attend such an endeavor, their families had to believe that education was key, and that was a notion that didn't exist in all immigrant families. The families also had to enjoy a big enough income so that the household did not require the children to contribute. And that narrowed the field considerably. For many of the hollow's families to stay afloat, many of their children went to work—in factories, shining shoes, or peddling newspapers.

Prior to the mid-1800s, reliance on such organizations or on charities such as the missionary society—or professionals (attorneys, doctors, and the like) in general—was minimal. Before education reform, people were expected to provide for their own education and medical care. Manuals on topics as varied as legal procedure and education were printed in greater and greater quantity and served as a kind of people's college. Paper was cheaper than it had been in years, and improvements in publishing delivered more and more how-to books to a growing populace hungry for information. While Frog Hollow was enjoying an unprecedented industrial boom, its newest residents—and not just the children among them—were casting about for new ways to learn.

Authors of medical pamphlets were sometimes trained physicians, and sometimes simply laypeople who had an interest in healthy living.

Catharine E. Beecher, Harriet Beecher Stowe's oldest sister, fell into the latter group. Before her sister gave voice to the voiceless with *Uncle Tom's Cabin*, Catharine Beecher, a staunch education reformer, wrote 1855's version of a bestseller with "Letters to the People on Health and Happiness." Known best for her treatises on domesticity and for her efforts to reform education, Beecher submitted her manuscript for publication only after she sent the pages to (female) experts to make sure propriety was observed on all topics. The book is arranged in a series of letters and calls for abandoning what Beecher—never one to mince words—called "family or quack medicines, unguided by medical science and skill."[32] As for her own health regimen, Beecher was a fan of the water cure—hydrotherapy—for pretty much every ailment, including stomachaches, chills, and constipation. In an 1850 letter to the *Courant*, Beecher encouraged the "scientific use of cold water," which should not be employed even by "medical men till they have read the standard works on the subject"—namely, her own writing. (Catharine Beecher was nothing if not sure of herself.) The water had to be pure and the medical care impeccable in order for the treatment to be effective—as it would be, against "all chronic diseases."[33]

Some of that same advice was found in early American almanacs such as those printed by Babcock and company. They began as one more way to deliver the Puritan orthodoxy, but almanacs morphed into compilations of the wisdom of the day. Latter-day almanacs became part medical and legal textbook, and part gossip magazine. Medical advertisements, which later included the quack cures so reviled by Beecher, began showing up in the 1830s. Though the early heavy hand of Puritanism was lifted somewhat by the early 1800s, an 1821 copy of *The Christian Almanac for Connecticut* was "devoted chiefly to the subject of Mission to the Heathens" and was loaded with essays in favor of temperance.[34]

In a direct way, technology driving Frog Hollow's engine also

Catharine Beecher. Courtesy of the Harriet Beecher Stowe Center, Hartford, Connecticut

brought with it a need for better education—something that went beyond a reliance on almanacs. Immigration increased, but new jobs required skills not always found among the neighborhood's newest residents. Women and children could find work as domestic help, but the men, particularly those who'd not had sufficient education in their countries of origins, often lost jobs to better-trained German and English immigrants.

Social reformers recognized the need for new residents to learn American ways, and Frog Hollow offered ample opportunities for immigrants to do so. Organizations such as the North American Civil League of Immigrants offered lessons in acclimation, including English classes, and lessons on how to avoid scams, which was always a concern for a population drawn to the promise of streets laid with gold. Such organizations' real purpose, however, was to "educate them and protect them from the malignant influences of social and industrial agitators."[35] The Civil League was created in 1907 by Frances Kellor, a reformer who believed that swift assimilation was the best antidote for immigrants who might be coming to do radical things, such as organize labor unions or push for a different form of government.[36] Frog Hollow residents who'd moved from Italy could troop downtown to the Hartford National Bank building, where interpreters walked them through the naturalization process. Polish immigrants had their own quarters on Sheldon Street.[37] Prior to the league, naturalization was generally conducted by the labor unions, with mixed results. Immigrants who couldn't read—about a sixth of the entire immigrant population—could attend English lessons at Brown School.[38]

In 1909 the Connecticut Daughters of the American Revolution hired a writer to prepare a manual specifically for Italian immigrants.[39] That same year, Dr. Peter Roberts, industrial secretary of the YMCA's international committee on immigration, told a crowd at Hartford's Jewell Hall that 75 percent of the immigrants coming to neighborhoods like Frog Hollow were immigrating from the same southeastern part of Europe. People were flocking to the Northeast—15 percent of the country was absorbing 83 percent of the immigrant population, said Roberts.[40]

Social service organizations in their infancy worked hard to offer one-stop shopping for immigrants in need, but the bulging population strained the city's capacity to care for them, and the responsibility of acclimating and educating increasingly fell to the schools. Children might arrive speaking little English, but they would be taught to go home and teach their parents. That was not always a successful method of acclimating parents.

On Babcock Street, what is now a school named for seasoned politician Maria Sánchez was once St. Anne's School, which had served as an anchor for the French Canadian children in the area run by the Sisters of the Holy Spirit beginning in the mid-1930s. The flock was overseen by a priest who'd walk down Park Street with his hands clasped behind his back, and when he passed a bar where he noticed a parishioner, he'd take a quarter from his pocket and rap on the window.

By the time St. Anne's School closed in 1987, the student population—mostly Vietnamese and Hispanic—was a perfect reflection of the changing neighborhood.[41] After 1970 it was impossible to pretend that members of Hartford's Hispanic and Latino communities were strictly there as seasonal workers. Drawn to a growing Spanish-speaking business community along Park Street, the community was growing and building a political power base. What would become Hartford's largest demographic (now edging toward 50 percent of the city's population) required that the city make some investment in their schools, their streets, and their neighborhoods.

By 1970 Frog Hollow was overwhelmingly—70 percent—Hispanic, 18 percent African American, and about 7 percent Caucasian. In an essay written by longtime *Hartford Courant* writer Tom Condon, the racial shift could be measured best in one old Park Street bar, the White Swan, which according to Condon drew "lawyers, artists, cops, musicians, students, singles, even the lieutenant governor," as well as Hispanic/Latino newcomers. A traditional restaurant, the Bean Pot, which had served the French Canadians in the neighborhood, added *sofritos* and rice and beans to the menu.

When a neighborhood is the victim of generations of disinvestment, the damage first strikes the most vulnerable. That means schools and their children are the canaries in the coal mine. As the neighborhood changed, students in Frog Hollow found themselves attending schools such as Burns School—now Burns Latino Studies Academy—that produced increasingly low test scores. Nationally, their fate was all but sealed in 1974 by the Supreme Court case *Milliken v. Bradley*, known in the press as the School Busing Case. Detroit parents and the NAACP in Detroit filed a lawsuit against then-governor William Milliken. They charged that the city had become segregated because of a series of illegal public policies (such

One of multiple protests at Burns School in the 1990s, this one to keep a school annex open. Photo by Stephen Dunn. Courtesy of the *Hartford Courant*

as redlining neighborhoods) and that students were suffering.[42] In Detroit the board of education "made segregation more pronounced by busing black students" to black schools, regardless of whether predominantly white schools were closer.[43]

The lower courts sided with the parents and the NAACP, but upon appeal the Supreme Court voted 5–4 to reject the idea of busing across school district lines. The Court said that "with no showing of significant violation by the 53 outlying school districts and no evidence of any inter-district violation or effect," busing was "wholly impermissible." The decision also said that the landmark school segregation case, *Brown v. Board of Education*, had no bearing on the case. School districts, the Court said, must maintain local control.[44] Local control has long been a battle cry in the Nutmeg State. Talks of regionalization—sharing resources such as emergency services—never get very far. The same holds true for schools.

Supreme Court justice Thurgood Marshall, the NAACP's chief

legal counsel for *Brown*, dissented. He wrote in *Milliken* that African American children were "intentionally confined to an expanding core of all-Negro schools" and that such segregation denied "the right of all of our children, whatever their race, to an equal start in life."[45] If all children could not go to school together, he wrote, how would they learn to live together?[46] The *Milliken* decision, according to a 2015 report on desegregation in Connecticut, made it "virtually useless to fight for metropolitan desegregation in the federal courts."[47]

But some families fought anyway. In April 1989 Elizabeth Horton Sheff and ten other families—among them eighteen school-age children—filed suit against the state of Connecticut in an effort to correct the racial, ethnic, and economic isolation of students in Hartford public schools. In 1991, as the court case got rolling, minority students made up 92.4 percent of Hartford's school population. The suit named as defendants then-governor William O'Neill, then-commissioner of education Gerald N. Tirozzi, then-state treasurer Francisco Borges, then-comptroller J. Edward Caldwell, and several members of the state board of education.

According to the suit, students in Hartford's poor schools were subject to "less-qualified teachers, insufficient supply of books for students, crumbling and poorly maintained buildings and lack of valuable learning tools such as science labs"—poor-quality education, in other words.[48]

After ten long years, well after many of the students had already graduated, the state Supreme Court ruled in favor of the plaintiffs. By then Hartford schools were educating a student body in which nearly 96 percent checked a box next to a minority designation. Racial segregation in the capital city schools was at an all-time high.[49] *Sheff* was one of the few such cases decided on state and not federal law, but the court offered a ruling and no remedy. The segregation was ruled to be de facto, not de jure, or by law. Had the segregation been ruled to have occurred because of the law, there would have been

Milo and Elizabeth Horton Sheff. Courtesy of the *Hartford Courant*

Connecticut state education commissioner Gerald N. Tirozzi. Courtesy of the *Hartford Courant*

federal remedies. How do you fix segregation that has occurred over generations?

The case became the equivalent of a cosmic Ping-Pong ball. Despite multiple court rulings and legal admonishments, Hartford—and Frog Hollow—schools remain heavily segregated. The lead plaintiff, Milo Sheff, eventually graduated from an alternative school and went to college to study engineering, art, and film. He also has performed as a rapper. Among his work:

> It started in '89
> April to be exact
> when questions
> arised
> concerning whites and blacks
> and unequal education
> and areas that
> lacked attention
> cause kids in this area are trapped.

Today, Burns Latino Studies Academy is a school with much room for improvement. A recent report from the State Department of Education says half the students are not proficient in English, roughly 80 percent are Hispanic, and less than 2 percent of sixth-graders met the state Connecticut Mastery Test goal in mathematics.[50]

6. Each Man and Woman

THE REVEREND PENNINGTON IS FREE

In 1850 the U.S. Congress passed the Fugitive Slave Act, much to the disgust of the editors at the *Courant*, who urged the North to ignore the "most ignoble" act: "Let every effort be made, at every subsequent election, by union and conciliation, so to elect our Representatives and Senators in Congress, so that such a law shall be repealed. We wish no employment of force. The law stands on the Statute Book and must be observed. But it must be wiped off from that book by all legal and constitutional means that we can employ."[1]

The Fugitive Slave Act required citizens to return escaped slaves to the people who purported to own them. This attempt at a compromise was problematic on every level. For people who opposed slavery, it required them to do something against their beliefs. And the act denied escapees due process. Abolitionists called it the Bloodhound Law after the dogs used to track down escaped people.[2] In reaction the Connecticut legislature passed a law meant to reduce the incidences of kidnappings and false imprisonments on the part of people who claimed slaves they didn't actually own. The *Courant* reported: "A real owner of a slave who comes to Connecticut, and by fair and honest methods and testimony reclaims his slave under the Fugitive Slave Act of 1850, has nothing to fear from our Connecticut law. When rogues, perjurers and kidnappers come here, and by

FALSE and MALICIOUS representations endeavor to prove that a free person entitled to freedom is a slave, they commit a high crime and misdemeanor, for which our law provides adequate punishment."[3] The punishment for anyone who sought to remove an enslaved person or provide false testimony to help remove an enslaved person was a five thousand dollar fine and up to five years in jail.

Into that world stepped Frog Hollow resident James W. C. Pennington, who was born into slavery in eastern Maryland as Jim Pembroke, according to an autobiography written by John Hooker, a Hartford lawyer. Before we explore Pennington's life, it's necessary to put Hooker into context. Hooker was a descendent of the Reverend Thomas Hooker, and he was married to the suffragist Isabella Beecher Hooker. Long before it was a polite thing to do, Hooker embraced "whole-souled abolition"—freedom from slavery that included complete enfranchisement of the people who had been owned by other people, including the right to vote and the right to own property. He embraced this belief even before his more famous in-laws, including Harriet Beecher Stowe. For his time, then, Hooker was a radical, and he was advised by colleagues to soft-pedal his abolitionism. Hooker later said his outspokenness might have slowed his career in the beginning, but he reached a level of respectability that allowed him to be considered for a seat on the state Supreme Court.

While Hooker was growing up in relative privilege in Farmington, Conn., Pennington/Pembroke was suffering the atrocities of a life lived in slavery. At age eleven Pennington was apprenticed to learn blacksmithing in Maryland, where he earned a reputation as an expert. As much as his blacksmithing skills brought him a measure of autonomy, Pennington was still a slave. At age eighteen or twenty (the record is not clear) he escaped after witnessing his father, Brazil Pembroke, being severely beaten by the man who owned the family. Pennington was beaten as well, but he said his father's pain and humiliation moved him to leave.

James W. C. Pennington.

"I never was a Slave after that," Pennington wrote.[4]

Pennington made his way to southern Pennsylvania, where he was taken in by Quakers anxious to help him transition to freedom—or as much freedom as society would allow. He learned to read and write, and made his way to Brooklyn, where he worked as a coachman and continued his studies. He began to speak in front of African American groups, and he spoke out against the American Colonization Society, an odd organization whose members thought the answer to slavery was to release the slaves and send them "back" to Africa. That many of the people who were enslaved had been here for generations and had scant connection with the continent was not a deterrent. More on that later.

Pennington campaigned for black parents to demand academic excellence from their children, which included parents pushing for their children to go to college.[5] He found his passion in ministry, and the self-educated man moved to New Haven to take over a church in the 1830s. In 1838 he performed the marriage of the social reformer

Frederick Douglass. In the year 1840, when the Census counted 263 slaves in Hartford, Pennington became minister of what is now Hartford's Faith Congregational Church.[6]

Hooker met the Reverend Pennington in 1844. Pennington's former owner, Frisby Tilghman, had found him, and Tilghman wanted his property back as he was anxious to take advantage of Pennington's legendary blacksmithing skills. Northern friends suggested Pennington go to Canada, where the economy was not as dependent on slavery and where he might find people to hide him. Meanwhile, Hooker, as his attorney, wrote Tilghman to ask for the man's freedom. "The ungrateful servant in whose behalf you write, merits no clemency from me," wrote Tilghman in early 1846. "He was guilty of theft when he departed, for which I hope he has made due amends."[7]

Buying his own freedom was beyond Pennington's budget, and so his supporters suggested he move farther away, to England. He did, and toured Europe and continued his studies. While visiting Germany, Pennington earned a doctorate of divinity, which he received with a gracious speech that he was accepting as a representative of his race, according to Hooker.

When the Fugitive Slave Law was passed, Pennington's return to Hartford seemed even less likely. He stayed in contact with Hooker and wrote to tell him that friends in Scotland had decided to raise money to purchase Pennington's freedom. He asked Hooker to contact Tilghman, who they found had died since his last letter. An administrator wrote back asking for $150. As executor of the will, Tilghman's representative said he could not grant manumission—freedom—to Pennington, so in order for all the t's to be crossed and the i's dotted, someone had to take possession of Pennington.

Joseph Hawley, who among his many other positions was John Hooker's law partner, took the sum to Maryland, and upon Hooker's request had the bill of sale made out to Hooker. "I thus became a slaveholder," wrote Hooker, "and the owner of a doctor of divinity."[8]

Joseph Hawley, abolitionist, governor, member of both the U.S. House of Representatives and the U.S. Senate, and former *Courant* owner/editor. Courtesy of the *Hartford Courant*

He held the bill for a day, he said, to see what it felt like, and the next day, June 5, 1851, he executed a deed of manumission, recorded in volume 76, page 356 of Hartford's town records. When Pennington returned to the United States, he came to Hartford to thank his supporters. At the gathering, he called up some who had been standing in the crowd. Hooker stepped onto the stage and joked that since a slave could own nothing, he decided to retain the doctorate of divinity when he released Pennington, and asked that people call him the "Rev. Dr. Hooker" henceforth.

During his time in Europe, the Reverend Pennington raised money by selling his home on Village Street. When he returned for good, he found rental property on Baker Street in Frog Hollow. At the time, his street was home to 20 families, three of whom were African American.[9]

Connecticut has long had a better reputation than it deserves when it comes to the institution of slavery. Northern states like Connecticut were not necessarily entirely abolitionist. Even when activists and advocates pushed to end slavery in the state, Connecticut's slave laws did not go down easily. The economy was built on slavery, and everyone (white) benefited from the economic boost that came from the building and outfitting of slave ships, or from ways far more subtle.[10] The newspaper-owning Babcocks did not own slaves, but the newspaper they ran certainly benefited from the institution. Scattered throughout its pages were advertisements that sought to find runaways—people who were enslaved, and people who had been apprenticed and wanted out of their arrangement either to escape abuse or to find better-paying work. From a January 26, 1801, *Mercury* ad:

> Run away from the subscriber in the night following the 25th inst. Levi Treat, in the 19th year of his age an indented apprentice, about 5 feet 8 or 9 inches high, dark complexion, dark hair; took with him a short Blue Jacket, one pair Blue Overalls, one Red Spotted Vest, two check Shirts, two pairs Stockings, one wool Hat, and many other articles not enumerated. Whoever will return said Levi to the subscriber shall receive 25 cents, but no charges paid.
>
> *Justus Blin*
>
> N.B. All persons are hereby forbid harboring, trusting, concealing or carrying away said Levi on penalty of the law.[11]

And in 1783, from the *Courant:*

> RUN away from the subscriber last night, a NEGRO LAD, named FRANK, about nineteen years old, a likely well made fellow, rather short—it is supposed he had on a blue broadcloth Coat, but may change it as he took sundry other Coats and small Cloathing with him—he formerly belonged to Mr. Alexander Hunt, and went off in company with a white Boy, about 16 years old, named George Graves—Whoever will take up said Negro and return him to the subscriber, shall be paid Ten Dollars and all reasonable charges.

The letter is signed Ebenezer Platt of Hartford.[12] A 1994 book, "Pretends to Be Free: Runaway Slave Advertisements from Colonial and Revolutionary New York and New Jersey," charts the breadth and depth of ads that promised swift retribution to anyone aiding and abetting a runaway.[13] Without touching a whip or a chain, newspaper owners benefited financially from keeping people enslaved. This was particularly true in Connecticut, which was never a hotbed of the abolitionist fervor that would overtake some of the rest of the nation. In fact, William Lloyd Garrison once called the state the "Georgia of New England."[14] While other states geared up for abolition, Canterbury, Connecticut, residents threw animal feces down the well of Prudence Crandall's school for African American girls and then prevented her from seeking a water source elsewhere.

Just before the Revolution, Connecticut was home to 6,464 slaves, more than any other New England state. People who owned people included the landed gentry, doctors, public officials, and ministers—in other words, respectable citizens. In 1784, after much discussion, Connecticut legislators passed a gradual emancipation rule. Gradual emancipation allowed slave owners, over time, to disconnect themselves from a slave economy, and it put the responsibility for freedom on the people who were enslaved.[15] In 1790 a census counted 263 slaves in Hartford. Documents found in the papers of a former tax collector in Hartford showed that slaves in 1815 were property to be taxed.[16] Great Britain abolished slavery in 1833, and in that same year, to appease angry residents concerned about the free slaves who would be living in their towns as a result of gradual emancipation, Connecticut legislators passed a law that banned students of color from attending school in the state without permission of local authorities.[17] The law was meant to counter the work of Crandall, who today is Connecticut's state heroine.

The state's method of emancipation was "protracted and idiosyncratic," according to a 2001 *Yale Law Journal* article.[18] Connecticut's

Gradual Abolition Act of 1784 gave a nod to the notion that slavery was wrong, but only a nod. It promised freedom on the twenty-fifth birthday (for men) or twenty-first birthday (for women) of the children who were born into slavery after March 1, 1784. The parents and grandparents of those children lived and died in slavery, unless the families who claimed to own them had a change of heart. Still, at a critical time years later, no less a person than President Abraham Lincoln supported gradual emancipation. A March 7, 1862, notice in the *Daily Courant* carried a message from the president that encouraged the acceptance of states where residents wanted to ease into freedom: "In my judgment, gradual and not sudden emancipation is better for all. In the more financial or pecuniary view any member of Congress, with the census tables and the treasury reports before him, can readily see for himself how very soon the current expenditures of this war would purchase at a fair valuation all the slaves in any named States."[19]

Early supporters of gradual abolition included Noah Webster, who worried that people who had been enslaved were not equipped to handle freedom, and that an incremental release would "prevent the distress of any sudden readjustment."[20] In a 1793 tract, Webster walked readers through the lives of the slaves of Turkey (who according to him sat around all day with pipes in their mouths), of Greece (deceitful, treacherous, and mean), and the "Moors" (given to robbery and piracy). "Slavery," he wrote, "corrupts the heart"—of both the slaver and the enslaved. Then, too, there were the slavers to consider, he said. To immediately abolish slavery, wrote Webster, would be to "reduce perhaps 20,000 white families to beggary." It would also encourage the recently enslaved to revolt. The only answer, he wrote, was to "raise, by gradual means, [the enslaved] to the condition of free tenants."[21]

As might be expected, enslaved African Americans were by and large willing to risk a "sudden readjustment," and in Hartford some engaged the services of (white) attorneys to fight for their freedom. Frog Hollow at the time had a sizable population of African Americans on its easternmost streets, the area closest to downtown Hartford. Gradual emancipation, for them, was a preservation of the status quo, with freedom coming only after decades in slavery, and freedom denied entirely to most adults.[22]

In a tradition that may have started as a way to quell potential riots among slaves, for years African Americans in Hartford held annual mock elections for a "governor" to preside over their social activities. The governor was strictly ceremonial but was given a riotous inauguration, nevertheless.[23] The election was generally held the Saturday after the regular election, when white men exercised their right to vote. Though voting was done by proxy, early on, "the choice was largely left to the masters, who chose a black for governor who was able to keep his fellows in order by means of his super intelligence and great muscular strength. Sometimes, the existing black governor passed his office and authority on to another of his own choice, but above all, the whites required that the black governor should be one notable for his honesty.

The governor would then appoint an entire staff, including a justice of the peace. Whatever the title of the member of the mayor's "staff," his real role was that of enforcer. One justice of the peace known as Squire Nep, a barber, was particularly brutal in meting out punishment. Early on, a magistrate named Jonathan Bull sent a black thief to Squire on some infraction. Squire ruled the man guilty and administered thirty lashes across his bare back, a punishment administered by dark of night on the town's South Green.[24]

For all its checkered emancipation history, Connecticut was home to its fair share of abolitionist heroes, including Crandall, Stowe, and John Brown, a native of Torrington. Organizations dedicated to abolition sprang up in and around Hartford, including the Connecticut Society for the Promotion of Freedom and the Relief of Persons

Unlawfully Holden in Bondage (though most of their members favored gradual emancipation). Even Stowe, known for advancing the cause of abolition with her classic, *Uncle Tom's Cabin*, couldn't envision a society where races shared power immediately. If you've read her book, it ends with a popular solution of the day, of colonizing people who had been enslaved. This solution was shared by many of her famous siblings and her father, the Reverend Lyman Beecher, and was promoted by the American Colonization Society, which included among its membership slaveholders as well as abolitionists. A Hartford society auxiliary was formed in 1819 after meeting at a local Episcopal church. Members were expected to pay at least one dollar a year and serve as a support to the larger organization. The purpose, according to the group's constitution, was to establish

> colonies upon the Western Coast of Africa, to restore, by their own consent, the free people of Colour in America, to the bosoms of their own kindred and people, and to the luxuriant soil of their own country; to give them freedom, and the lights of science and the Gospel; to dispel the gloom of paganism, and the grossest idolatry, from the benighted regions of Africa, by unfurling the banner of the cross; to raise the sons of Africa to their proper rank in the scale of intellectual existence; to encourage and ultimately to produce an entire emancipation of the slaves in America; and last, though not least—to break up and destroy that inhuman and accursed traffic, the SLAVE TRADE—the offspring of avarice, and all the viler passions of the human heart.[25]

By 1830 the annual meeting of the state Colonization Society was sponsoring Sermon Sundays, when clergy were encouraged to spread the word about the work of the group. The benefits of removing former slaves to Africa, according to an 1830 *Courant* article, were every bit as paternalistic as Noah Webster's support of gradual emancipation. Colonization would keep former slaves from sinking "into vice and indolence and ruin; and contaminate the slave population; and thus render their future emancipation the more difficult and hopeless."[26] The article also included accounts of other attempts at colonization from Great Britain and the West Indies, though results were mixed at best.

For its proponents, colonization would serve two purposes: it would remove from the country the people who'd been enslaved, and it would assume that those Christianized people (the people who'd been enslaved, many of whom were Muslim and had been converted or coerced to Christianity) could be counted on to spread the Gospel to non-Christians in Africa. As for convincing freed American slaves to move to the far-off land, the tract said planners anticipated no difficulty.

In fact Pennington wasn't alone in his opposition to colonization. African American leaders of the abolition movement, including Douglass, opposed it. In Douglass's *North Star* newspaper the abolitionist called colonization the "twin sister of slavery" and argued that people who had been enslaved had earned the right to call the United States their native land. For centuries, Douglass wrote, the African had "toiled over the soil of America, under a burning sun and a driver's lash—ploughing, planting, reaping, that white men might loll in ease."[27] Who better to claim ownership of that land—or at least a piece of it?

Despite the opposition to emigration (which grew in Hartford in the 1830s), the national society settled some thirteen thousand people in Liberia before it stopped emigrations in 1913 and legally disbanded in 1964. As Douglass and others pointed out, colonization was not a workable policy. People who'd emigrated sent back stories of their challenges, while African Americans in Connecticut, with their fortunes improving at home, saw no reason to pick up and leave for the unknown of Africa. Eventually, only slave owners supported colonization.

Meanwhile, the Underground Railroad was secreting people north through Hartford. Farmington, located west of Hartford, is known as Connecticut's Grand Central Station for the railroad, but Hartford had its share of safe havens and one was just northwest of Frog Hollow in the barn of Francis Gillette, a former U.S. senator and neighbor of Stowe (and Mark Twain).

Starting in 1841, African American residents petitioned for the right to vote in Connecticut. In 1843, 115 black residents presented a petition to the General Assembly, but the petition went nowhere until 1846, when legislators set a referendum to remove the word "white" from the state constitution. The referendum was crushed, 19,148 to 5,253.[28] Eventually, even cautious Connecticut had to admit that gradual emancipation was taking too long, and in 1848 the state legislators eliminated the process by passing a law that said "no person shall hereafter be held in slavery in this State."[29]

The shift was significant but mostly only in a legal sense. Charles S. Johnson, National Urban League director of research and investigation, who studied Hartford's African American population in the early 1920s, wrote that old New Englanders' view of black residents early on was "paternalistic and kindly."[30] As Johnson wrote, by 1850 all of the people who'd been enslaved in Hartford were freed, yet many remained attached (mostly economically) to the city's wealthier families. If relations were cordial on the surface, away from their employers the African American community by necessity operated in another world. Churches, barbershops, and liveries served the black communities, with little to no comment or contribution from the white community. That paternalistic attitude served as a great limiter to African American success. Only a crisis that called for a new workforce—World War I—would help the struggle for enfranchisement, said Johnson.

Even when it came to fighting for their own freedom, African Americans were treated as an afterthought. Only in the third year of the Civil War were black soldiers in Connecticut permitted to enlist. After the Emancipation Proclamation in 1863, enlistment increased to an estimated 700,000 new black troops, some of whom were already free.[31] Then, in May 1863, the U.S. Department of War's General Order No. 143 established the Bureau of Colored Troops. An opportunity to belong to the military was vital for full enfranchisement, according to some of the leading abolitionists of the day. Said Frederick Douglass, "Once let the black man get upon his person the brass letters, U.S., let him get an eagle on his button, and a musket on his shoulder, and bullets in his pockets, and there is no power on earth which can deny that he has earned the right to citizenship in the United States."[32]

Connecticut legislators did not act until that November, when two Republican legislators from New Haven introduced a bill that organized Connecticut black regiments. Democrats in the state balked because they worried that the new troops would not observe the decorum of war, and might instead wreak havoc on Southerners. But the Democrats were outnumbered. Legislators could not, however, agree on remuneration. As an enticement for enlisting, black soldiers were offered $310 from the state, $75 from the county, and $300 from the federal government. By way of comparison, at the time a pound of coffee cost less than one dollar, and a decent home could be purchased in Frog Hollow for one thousand dollars.[33] Beyond the attraction of fighting for one's freedom, the financial incentive was substantial, but as it turned out, the troops would only receive payment from the state—and then not in full. The soldiers' first paycheck wasn't the thirteen dollars per month they'd been promised, but seven dollars. They were advised to take the lesser amount without complaining, and most of them did.[34] Meanwhile, county and federal governments reneged on their part of the deal. And though President Abraham Lincoln and others, including Connecticut's senator Lafayette S. Foster, campaigned for equity, the wives and children of black soldiers who died while in service were often not awarded the same pension given to their white peers—or any pension at all. The legal loophole for this was maddening. The wives of black soldiers had mostly been married in slavery, and marriages performed in slavery were not recognized by the state.[35]

But none of this stopped the recruits. So many would-be soldiers showed up to enlist in New Haven that a second regiment—the Thirtieth—was organized.[36] The Twenty-Ninth included one thousand men, and they were among the two hundred thousand black soldiers who fought in the Civil War. Though the men were given a hearty send-off from New Haven, letters home showed that they were not always treated with respect—certainly not by Southerners anxious to maintain a slave economy, yet not always by Northerners who were against slavery on paper but uncomfortable with mingling.

The regiment mustered out to South Carolina and eventually to Texas, where water was in short supply and the men gratefully paid ten cents a canteen for water from the Rio Grande. They lost five hundred men on Virginia's battlefields, and some soldiers in the regiment were among the first to enter Richmond, the capital of the Confederacy, after the fall of that city in April 1865.[37] More than a few of those men came from the hollow.

In October 1865, when President Andrew Johnson greeted a colored regiment in Washington after the war, saying, "This is as much your country as anybody else's," the *Courant* chortled that the "Democratic" line of treating black residents as "dumb, driven cattle" would most assuredly have to stop.[38] The *Courant* carried a small notice on November 23, 1865, that the regiment was expected home and preparations were underway to give an "earnest welcome" to the soldiers who had "done their whole duty, and done it well."[39] The welcome home was delayed until a boat could be procured for the trip. When the troops—from the Twenty-Ninth and the Thirty-First—arrived on the steamers *City of Hartford* and *Granite State*, Governor William A. Buckingham greeted them with a speech:

> I welcome you from sleepless watchings, from fatiguing marches, from the privations of the camp, and from the dangers of the battlefield, to the rest, the pleasures and the duties which pertain to peace, to home, and civil life . . . and although Connecticut now denies you privileges which it grants to others, for no other apparent reason than because God has made you to differ in complexion, yet justice will not always stand afar off. Be patient; be true to yourselves. Remember that merit consist not in color or in birth, but in habits of industry, in intellectual ability and moral character. Show by your acquirements and your devotion to duty in civil life that you are as true to virtue and the interests of government and country, as you have been while in the army, and soon the voice of a majority of liberty-loving freemen will be heard demanding for you every right and every privilege to which your intelligence and moral character shall entitle you.[40]

In May 1869, Connecticut's Republican governor Marshall Jewell sent to the state Senate a copy of the Fifteenth Amendment, which granted the right to vote to black men. Thirteen Republicans voted yes, and six Democrats voted no. The amendment moved to the House, where after a two-hour debate legislators again mostly voted according to their party—126 Republicans in favor, and 104 Democrats against (with seven absentees). Just one state Republican representative, James C. Walkley, an insurance company president and railroad owner and a self-identified conservative from the strongly Democratic town of Haddam, crossed the party line to vote no. That aberration aside, Connecticut became the twenty-second state to ratify the amendment.

In February 1870 the U.S. Congress ratified the amendment, which was meant to grant civil rights to everyone regardless of "race, color, or previous condition of servitude." Only "after considerable and often acrimonious debate," the Connecticut General Assembly changed the state constitution to allow African American the vote, though voter intimidation and poll taxes continued to be barriers.[41] The amendment left out protection for women, and that consigned suffragists, including full-throated activists in Frog Hollow and Hartford, to another half century of lobbying for a vote of their own.

In 1871 the Twenty-Ninth Connecticut Volunteer Infantry and others celebrated with a downtown parade, a picnic, and an evening dance at Allyn Hall on Asylum Street. The speaker that day reminded the audience that "colored men have always been true to the Union."[42] But official emancipation wasn't complete for any black residents in Connecticut until long after the Civil War. The status enjoyed by Frog Hollow's African American residents "was, at best a quasi-freedom, hard won and easily lost."[43]

Scottish games were held on July 4, 1871, in what was still known as Penfield's Grove, at the corner of Zion and Park. The *Hartford Courant* noted that the setting offered delightful views of the mountain range to the west, and that attendees were fortunate as the groves were not often opened to the public by Penfield, who'd helped bring Sharps Rifle to town. He opened the groves again for a revival meeting of African American Christians in September 1879. The Reverend Essex Roberts, formerly of Washington, D.C., who was pasturing at the Calvary Church on Albany Avenue, was the speaker. The Reverend Roberts was described as a "tall, dignified man," and a stand was built and boards placed on tree stumps for pews. The Reverend Roberts attracted "comparatively few colored people," but "hundreds of white boys with a few gentlemen and ladies." The white boys had not come to worship but to heckle, being as the *Courant* reported, "full of life and only too ready to laugh at the least provocation of mirth." Roberts read from Hebrews 10, a rebuke of animal sacrifices, and asked the audience to stop laughing, as the gathering was "not a theater or minstrel show." The audience quieted down, but a week later the camp meeting disbanded. The Reverend Roberts wasn't able to get weekday attendance, and one Friday white lads took over the service to perform "an impromptu minstrel show." The *Courant* labeled them "Frog Hollow toughs." They were so loud that some neighbors came to investigate, but when they discovered the source of the noise, they left without intervening.

After the turn of the last century, the Great Migration brought African American families from Georgia, the Carolinas, and Virginia. Some came to work in the tobacco fields north of the city. Most of those families tended to stay only a short time, but in families where members were able to get a better-paying manufacturing job, the roots went deep and quick. From one study, the proportion of male black workers classified as "operatives" (or semiskilled workers) between 1940 and 1950 in the U.S. Census rose from 16.2 to nearly 24 percent. The movement of black men into manufacturing was a major component of the men's subsequent economic success.[44] In the same way, black women who worked in the defense industry found themselves farther up the economic ladder after World War II, due to their time spent on the factory floor.[45] By war's end, nearly a quarter of married black women were working in factories, answering telephones, or were in some way involved in the industrial war effort.[46]

The second phase of the Southern Diaspora started during World War II and continued into the 1970s. During that time, at least ten million southerners—roughly six million of them African American—left their home states for opportunities elsewhere, both the Midwest and the Northeast.[47] As Isabel Wilkerson wrote in her 2010 National Book Critics Circle Award-winning book, *The Warmth of Other Suns*, "From the early years of the twentieth century to well past its middle age, nearly every black family in the American South, which meant nearly every black family in America, had a decision to make."[48]

These migrants, wrote Wilkerson, were no different from people crossing the Atlantic or the Rio Grande. Their homeland, too, was by comparison an undeveloped country.[49] The poet Carl Sandburg wrote that the cities to which they were moving—among them Hartford and, more specifically, Frog Hollow—were "a receiving station and a port of refuge."[50]

As a receiving station, Hartford was better prepared for the influx than other midsized eastern cities, having served as a receiving station for roughly one hundred years already. By the early 1920s a small and vibrant African American business community included enterprises such as barbershops, beauty salons, groceries, music studios, restaurants, funeral parlors, billiard parlors, afterhours clubs, taxi services, and boarding houses. Moreland Barbershop offered an opportunity for hair grooming and conversation. Migration from the South clearly fostered some of that business growth, and at the same time it attracted more residents. Yet as with immigrant groups like the Italians and the Irish, the southern African Americans were rather quickly consigned to the role of miscreant—even northern-born African Americans sometimes tried to distance themselves from the newcomers.[51]

Earlier discussions about what to do with the city's newcomers had raged in the *Courant*. A June 1882 letter to the editor defended "the Russo-Jewish immigrants": "The male immigrants who have thus far arrived in this city have all been placed either on farms, in factories, or in mechanical and artisan employments. The women are set to work in factories or as domestics. So far from its being true that these immigrants will not take to agriculture, it is a fact that over one-half are eager to go upon farms, among them men who are physically unable to endure the work, but who hope to become inured to it by degrees."[52]

Other immigrant groups were still viewed with suspicion or worse. A *Popular Science* article from August 1906 reported soberly that homicides increased significantly in cities that welcomed Italian immigrants:

In New Haven, Connecticut, where the Italian population has greatly increased since 1890, the ratio of arrests for homicide has about doubled during the past six or eight years. In 1880, the ratio of arrests for murder and manslaughter in that city was 1.59 per 100,000 of inhabitants; in 1890, 2.46; and during the four years 1901–04 there were 4.16 arrests per 100,000 of population on the charge of killing a fellow man. This ratio is still quite low, compared with some cities of the east, but the increase is very significant, especially in view of the fact that the second generation of foreigners is always more criminally inclined than the first.[53]

The arguments hit at the heart of Frog Hollow. In June 1907 the debate club at Hartford High School, a school that drew students from the neighborhood, won a contest arguing against the statement that immigration should be restricted. First prize went to Paul Macy, who "closed for the negative, had a very forceful and racy speech, interspersed with many jokes and stories."[54]

The Church of the Immaculate Conception, today a part of ImmaCare Inc., an organization that seeks to prevent homelessness, was built in 1894 on Park Street. A year later, construction started on the graceful brick Lyceum, which is now home to the nonprofit Partnership for Strong Communities, another antihomelessness organization. The archdiocese hired John J. Dwyer, a well-known Hartford architect, to design the stately, three-story brick building on Lawrence Street. The church wanted a place for immigrant children to escape the streets, which were becoming increasingly challenging. The building included a basketball court and bowling lanes. The third floor contained a classroom dedicated to elocution lessons, meant to remove the brogue from the young Irish immigrants. The lessons didn't always take.

Frog Hollow streets, filled with a tapestry of non-English speakers, were sprinkled with the Irish accent. By 1910, 30 percent of the state's population was foreign-born.[55] The American Dream seemed available to anyone willing to work, although those willing to work were increasingly born elsewhere, making Frog Hollow the proverbial melting pot of ethnicities and languages. Prior to 1870 just two-hundred-some Italians were recorded in the entire state. By 1910 roughly seven thousand people of Italian descent called Hartford home.[56]

7. *Growing Weary and Mistrustful*

THE NEIGHBORHOOD GETS AN ORPHANAGE

With more residents came more challenges, particularly around keeping Hartford residents healthy. Epidemics had a way of taking the city by the neck and shaking it. In the early days, cholera ("the Cholera") was always a threat, and ignorance about the spread of the disease was rampant. People reached for whatever explanation was handy, and many times those explanations were not grounded in science or data but in fear of the newcomers. An 1849 *Courant* article explained that the Irish and the "blacks in the South" were more prone to suffer from communicable diseases because of the "poriferous structure of their skins," which, it was thought, not only favors "perspiration, but likewise admits the escape of animal effluvia, and when interrupted in its functions, exposes them at once to a danger of this kind."[1] This was one way of putting the spread of diseases squarely on the shoulders of the newest residents of Frog Hollow. No mention was made of contaminated water (cholera), and it would be a few years before anyone connected public sanitation policy with typhoid.[2]

By 1854 the *Courant* was home to long involved stories about the need for cleanliness: "Along the various mill ponds of the Little River into which the city sewers may carry impurities of the city, care should be taken to prevent the water from stagnating and thus retaining for weeks all the accumulated filth. Stables should be particularly watched and washed, and those generators of disease, hog-pens, should be banished from the city, at least during the summer months."[3]

Orphanages were unusual in colonial America. Children left alone by death or desertion had several options, and few of them were good. They might be absorbed into already-existing families, though that proved disastrous to some, who would be treated strictly as indentured servants, or worse, in agrarian Connecticut.[4]

The Hartford Orphan Asylum was part of a national reform movement to better deal with children without support. Such asylums were available to children who'd lost both parents and to children whose remaining parent proved incapable of supporting them. At times, even two-parent families would avail themselves of the services of orphanages and sign their children into the care of the institutions, which might then sign out those children to waiting families who agreed to teach the children in some industry (farming was popular) and then release them with a small stipend on their twenty-first birthday.

The asylum catered to the needs of Hartford boys, while Hartford girls were cared for by an organization called the Female Beneficent Society. The groups merged in 1865, and by 1879 they had outgrown their building and moved into new Queen Anne facilities set on a hill on Putnam Street. The new facility included day and night nurseries, which allowed staff to take in infants, something that was not done at the earlier facility.[5] As one of Hartford's most popular charities, the building housed 150 boys and girls, who ate together but—in a reflection of the thinking of the day—attended neighborhood schools off-campus to lessen the effects of institutionalization, according to the National Register of Historic Places. By the turn of the next century, attention had turned from congregate housing to cottage institutions, which trustees replicated on Putnam Street—first for girls, in 1911. The experiment worked well enough that the orphanage

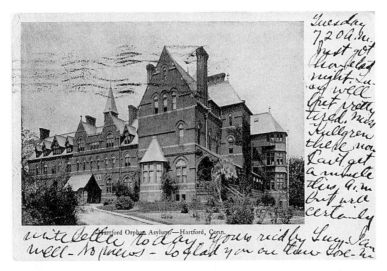

Hartford Orphan Asylum. Photo by George E. Wright. Richard L. Mahoney
Collection, Hartford History Center, Hartford Public Library

board bought land to the north, on Asylum Avenue, to build a new
facility. The Putnam Street orphanage was closed and eventually torn
down to make way for a neighborhood school.

Asylum Hill was also home to an almshouse for needy people.
Sometimes children were assigned to live there, much to the distress
of William Goodwin, a New Haven resident who took a tour of the
facilities in 1849 and wrote about the practice of housing criminals
and the poor (including children) in one structure. After writing
glowingly of the physical plant, Goodwin wound up:

> Some dozen or more of the "motley group" were actually committed
> thieves and vagabonds. Now, this is too bad; and what makes the
> matter the more heart-rending is to learn, that the latter class, are
> permitted to partake of their meals at the same table with the virtu-
> ous poor! Is this right? Should there be no difference made between
> crime and poverty, brought on perhaps, through unavoidable circum-

stances, to be insulted by being placed in the same room, and at the same table with thieves, and vagrants of the vilest description?—Poverty, sir, is neither a crime nor a sin.[6]

Another institution, the Hartford Home, opened in 1863 on Retreat Avenue as a place for children whose parents were on public relief but were not providing for the children. There, too, children could be indentured to families—the males until age twenty-one, the females until age eighteen—but the facility closed after seven years, when city officials investigated and found discipline lacking and no set program for training the children.[7]

For all the need for social services, in the middle-to-late 1800s the town had the smell of upward mobility with the highest per capita income in the country. Hartford boasted manufacturing and a growing publishing industry that at one point included twelve different publishing houses. Mark Twain came to town to be near his.

8. *They Are Innately Capable*

DOMINICK BURNS OPENS A BANK, AND MARIA

SÁNCHEZ SHEPHERDS A POLITICAL FORCE

Dominick F. Burns came to Hartford in 1857 as a ten-year-old Irish boy. He traveled with a card tied around his neck, so his relatives would recognize him. In 1877 he went to work at a meat store on Asylum Street, where he learned the art of selling—or more likely, enhanced his already impressive skills. On January 1, 1881, he formed a partnership, Cannon & Burns, with T. P. Cannon and opened a grocery and meat business at 304 Park Street alongside a doctor's offices and a laborers' temple. There he became known as the Saint of Park Street. Burns never let anyone leave his store empty-handed, no matter what the person's financial circumstances. He later bought out Cannon and in 1903 established a grocery store under the name D. F. Burns Co. on the corner of Park and Lawrence streets. His business eventually grew to twenty-five employees.

You have heard the Burns name before. Dominick Burns is the grandfather of writers John Gregory Dunne and Dominick Dunne, and the great-grandfather of actor and producer Griffin Dunne, who returns to Hartford to host fund-raisers for the school that bears his great-grandfather's name. Throughout his life, John Gregory Dunne, novelist, screenwriter, and raconteur, made frequent reference to Burns, his maternal grandfather, and to Frog Hollow. Dunne, accord-

ing to his 2004 *New York Times* obituary, also spent his writing life
"grappling with his own Irish Catholic background [which] yielded
searing literary glimpses into the sometimes-tormented experience
of Irish Americans."[1]

During his grandfather's life, Frog Hollow, wrote Dunne, was "a
community of male Irish laborers and female Irish domestics who
worked farther west in the households of people I still call, with a
special distaste not allayed by my years, Yanks; 'WASP' belongs to the
sanitized diction of pop anthology."[2] Despite his literary marriage to
Joan Didion, despite his Hollywood friendships and credits, he once
wrote that he remained "ineffably Frog Hollow."[3]

For years Burns's store was the epicenter of the neighborhood. One
day in 1896, a drunk came in, tried to pick a fight, and then grabbed
a meat cleaver and struck the butcher on the head. The attacker was
pinned to the ground by Burns's brother, James.[4]

Like the industrialists before him, Burns was anxious to expand
his kingdom. At the time, the neighborhood that had been so good
to him lacked a bank, so in 1920 Burns helped found the Park Street
Trust Company at the corner of Park and Broad streets, where he
served as its first president. It was one of some thirty thousand banks
in the country at the time. Public documents from that year show
that total assets, $724,499.16, matched total liabilities.

Banks such as Park Street were chartered to answer a crying need
among customers whom other banks would not serve. Larger banks
refused to administer loans to Roman Catholics, to Irish, to African
Americans, or to Jews. The last of these were never a large presence
in Frog Hollow, though they were numerous enough to bury their
dead in the neighborhood's Zion Hill Cemetery. Among others,
Congregation Ados Israel, a downtown synagogue that closed in
1986, maintained a plot there.

With the slogan "A Bank for the People," Burns's trust was the
only bank within a mile of the booming Park Street business district

that would serve any customer. Word got around. On the first day of business, the bank was festooned with flowers and the line stretched out the door.[5] On the fiftieth anniversary of Burns's arrival in the United States, employees and others sent fifty baskets of red roses.

The gratitude went beyond flowers. Catering to the growing foreign-born population made good sense. For such a small state, Connecticut had a fairly diverse population, and members of that population needed a place to put their money and get loans to reach toward the American Dream.[6] (Even today Connecticut has the fastest-growing and one of the largest populations of foreign-born residents in the country.)

In the early 1800s Ireland was enjoying relative prosperity, and incentive to leave was small. Then came massive population growth. At the start of that century, Ireland had roughly 2 million citizens. In a generation that figure leaped to 6.8 million. The Napoleonic Wars brought an economic slump in Europe and along with it a major collapse in most industries. Add to that a typhoid epidemic and weird weather patterns that damaged or destroyed a vast acreage of grain and potato crops.[7] The early wave of Irish immigrants were people like James Mooklar, an early Hartford barber. Early Irish immigrants were mostly skilled or semiskilled workers such as weavers, spinners, and the like.[8]

The second wave of Irish who immigrated to Hartford included political radicals who were "forced into exile because of their outspoken opposition to England's rule over Ireland."[9] The Catholics among them tended to be less willing to blend in, which gave birth to a new phrase, "Scotch-Irish," which was used to distinguish the Protestant Irish from the Catholic Irish.[10]

For Irish Catholics who had survived back-to-back calamities at home, immigration to the stony ground of New England was their only hope, though anti-Catholic rhetoric based in nativism that was long rooted in British culture was embedded in the national conversation. As far back as the early 1700s, the Irish Catholic was called "an idolater, who worships Images, Pictures, Stocks and Stones, the Works of Mens Hands; calls upon the Virgin Mary, Saints and Angels to pray for them; adores Reliques.... He ... prefers Traditions before the Holy Scriptures; thinks good Works alone merit Heaven, eats his God by the cunning Trick of Transubstantiation . . . ; and swears the Pope is infallible."[11]

This is a conversation familiar to students of recent history. Newcomers are labeled brutes and savages, and they are accused of taking jobs away from people who have been here for generations.[12] Early on, when most of the Irish immigrants were Protestant, the welcome was relatively warm, and when the number of Catholic immigrants remained small, Connecticut residents were at least somewhat accommodating. In 1813 the Roman Catholic priest Francis Matignon, of Boston, passed through Hartford one weekend and was kept from traveling on the Lord's Day—Sunday—by Puritan rules. The Reverend Matignon was invited to speak at Hartford's Center Church, where he was received as an honored guest. That response quickly gave way to fear and innuendo around Catholicism. The mouthpiece for much of the propaganda was the *Connecticut Observer*, a Hartford-based newspaper published from 1825 to 1839. A July 1829 *Observer* editorial worried when a publication meant for Catholics in Connecticut began printing. "How will it read in history, that in 1829, Hartford, in the State of Connecticut, was made the centre of a Roman Catholic mission?"[13]

As more Catholic immigrants came to Hartford and Frog Hollow, their religion was mocked as incompatible with American democracy. The Puritans reacted with "characteristic illiberality."[14] Considering conditions back in Ireland and the potential for a shot at the still-unnamed American Dream, Irish Roman Catholics were willing to chance it. Beginning in the 1820s, the Irish came to Connecticut to build canals in Farmington and Enfield, as well as tracks for the

New Haven and Hartford railroads. That meant that early Irish immigrants helped pave the way—or build the canal—that allowed for more immigrants to follow.[15] The Farmington Canal was meant to connect New Haven to Connecticut's interior and beyond, but an 1850 pamphlet said the company was "early crippled in their efforts, by the want of money."[16] Spring freshets kept collapsing the canal, and business owners concerned with interruption of services—which for all the freshets was still a rare occurrence—were reluctant to use the canals. When the venture failed, Irish immigrants switched to building railways that would help move industry into modern times. Their efforts laid the groundwork to set "the United States as a future industrial giant."[17]

Most of the new Irish Americans were too poor to buy land and so they moved to the cities. (Farm work required entire families, and most Irish were not only poor but alone as well. Their hope was in manufacturing centers, where jobs were plentiful.)[18] In 1835 a Catholic census showed 720 members of the faith in Connecticut. Within nine years, the number had jumped to 4,817. The Irish were coming at a propitious time. American party politics, long the playground of the rich and powerful, were changing.[19] City governments were taking shape. New jobs were created to handle the growing population.[20] Firefighters, police officers—all were positions that needed to be filled, and the Irish stepped in. (Over time, in Hartford, the Irish gravitated toward firefighting, while the Italians went to the police force.)

Frog Hollow's heyday mirrored the immigrant shift into Hartford, and the new residents needed places to worship as well. Churches sprang up, though the immigration of Roman Catholics into Connecticut was "noticeably different from that in other parts of the country in its relative lack of diversity."[21] Hartford had, for a time, six German parishes, but the Catholics in the city were predominantly Irish, followed by Italians and eastern Europeans.[22] Meanwhile, the

Irish with their churches and businesses and banks had made inroads in Waspy Connecticut. As a group, they had survived prejudice that took many forms, including that of a literacy test as a prerequisite for voting.[23] Immigrants rather quickly found a way around the law, which required literacy but didn't specify in what language. By 1870 more than half of the immigrants in the state were Irish born.[24] The historic Puritan distaste for Roman Catholicism lingered. A letter to the *Courant* editor on March 31, 1870, decried a "democratic war on Irish voters": "The democratic leaders have for years pretended to be special champions of the foreign element here, yet whenever to power they have gone back upon their profession and have been very careful to distribute all the spoils among themselves."[25]

By 1916 the *Hartford Courant* reported that people of Irish descent outnumbered all other ethnic groups in town and also held more political offices—that of mayor, fire chief, and police chief—than any other.[26] Over time the population in Frog Hollow shifted from Irish to Italian to French Canadian to Puerto Rican. In 1950 the population of Puerto Ricans on the mainland was about 226,000. By 1980 that number rose to nearly a million.[27] When the need for cheap labor declined in New York, it continued in Hartford.[28] In the 1970s, though manufacturing jobs were drying up, the city kept drawing "a continuing migration of poor people who settled despite shrinking economic opportunities."[29]

But even with the influx of new residents, the city was losing population.[30] Between 1950 and 1960 the city saw an outmigration of some fifteen thousand people, or about 9 percent of the town's residents. By 1970 that figure had increased to 11 percent.[31] And where were they going? To the suburbs, which were waiting to greet them with relatively affordable homes, schools that were on the rise, and manufacturers who would move to towns that offered them tax incentives.[32] Families with more resources could pick up and move from a city that was said to be dying. They took their energy and their taxes and applied them to the towns surrounding Hartford. West Hartford, just to the west, went from a population of 44,402 in 1950, to 62,382 in 1960, to 68,031 in 1970.

Call it white flight, though Hartford remained a white-majority city until 1990.[33] Such a draining of resources is a recipe for disaster for any city, and it came to fruition in Frog Hollow in many forms, including highly organized gangs bent on acquiring turf for their illegal activities. Within a generation, quelling gang activity required the full force of the federal government. Only one gang, Park Street Posse, did not deal in weaponry and was more prone to hold car washes than fight over turf.[34] The others were far more threatening and were devoted to battle for supremacy in drug dealing in the old neighborhood. Longtime and recent neighbors not involved in gang activity watched as Frog Hollow became a violent battlefield in the drug wars. Gang activity became noticeable in the 1970s and declined in the '80s, but came roaring back in the '90s.[35]

Frog Hollow was now overwhelmingly Hispanic (70 percent), 18 percent African American, and 7 percent Caucasian. At the time, the Hispanic population in the rest of Hartford was mostly of Puerto Rican origin. Many were refugees from the sugar wars in Puerto Rico, when large U.S. corporations took over the industry and squeezed small farmers out.[36] By 1940 the world sugar industry relied almost entirely on U.S. consumption, and that reliance would only grow deeper over the next few decades. When the United States suffered a recession in the 1970s, the island's economy tanked. Many of Connecticut's seasonal workers decided to brave the New England winters, and those who'd planned to leave after tobacco-picking ended, stayed.

While Connecticut was becoming home to more people of color, the state's legislators were moving to decentralize power in the state, and that would have a huge impact on newer residents. In 1960 Connecticut legislators voted to abolish county governments. By then, county governments—never a big source of power in the state—had limited power, but their abolishment further localized decision-making in each of the state's 169 towns and created what amounted to 169 fiefdoms. It also created an environment for rampant duplication of services such as fire and police, school boards, and the like.

By the late 1960s, many of the families who had migrated from Puerto Rico lived in Hartford's South Green area, but then urban renewal projects, highway construction, and the expansion of institutions such as Hartford Hospital moved many of those families to other neighborhoods, including Frog Hollow. The same tropes trotted out for generations of newcomers who were immigrating were trotted out again for the migrants from Puerto Rico, and white flight sped up—though there was a significant cohort of longtime residents who vowed to stay, and vowed to be neighborly.

Maria Clemencia Colón Sánchez moved to Hartford from her native Puerto Rico to work in the tobacco fields north of town. She did not have much in the way of a formal education, but Sánchez began educating herself about the politics of the capital city. She owned a candy store/newsstand in the North End that was more of a social service agency than a store, according to an unpublished thesis by *Philadelphia Daily News* columnist Helen Ubiñas. Hispanic and Latino leaders, along with other city leaders, began to meet in the store to discuss the gaps in services for the community. One of Sánchez's first battles was to get a Spanish-speaking priest at her church, Sagrado Corazón (Sacred Heart). The wave of people moving north from Puerto Rico gave rise to a new brand of politicians. In 1973 Maria Sánchez, for whom one of Frog Hollow's schools is named, set her sights on a seat on the Court of Common Council (Hartford's town council). She was discouraged by Democratic Party leaders because, they said, she spoke English with a heavy accent. Sánchez didn't have the full support of the leadership, but she was already considered the godmother (*la madrina*) in her own commu-

Maria Clemencia Colón Sánchez, "La Madrina," member of the Hartford school board, and a Connecticut state representative. Courtesy of the *Hartford Courant*

nity. When a party leader suggested to another Puerto Rican pol a different candidate, that candidate told him to go to hell.[37] Sánchez was better prepared.

Sánchez became the first Puerto Rican on Hartford's board of education in what the *Hartford Courant* said was the cheapest campaign ever financed by the town Democratic committee. Sánchez's campaign cost just $910. There is something to be said for grassroots support. She organized and was elected treasurer of the town's new Puerto Rican Democrats of Hartford in 1965. She also served as a liaison between police and rioting Hispanics concerned with aggressive police activity in their neighborhood.[38] She was elected to the Hartford board of education in 1973; in 1988 she again broke a barrier for Hispanic women when she was elected to the state General Assembly.

In addition Sánchez helped create a variety of social service and social justice agencies in the city, including (but not limited to) La Casa de Puerto Rico, the Society of Legal Services, the Spanish-

American Merchants Association, the Puerto Rican Businessmen Association, and the Community Renewal Team. She organized an annual Puerto Rican parade (under the slogan "Register and Vote").[39] She pushed for mandatory bilingual education in the city's schools, though she hadn't gone past eighth grade herself.

At her candy store, wrote Ubiñas, Sánchez kept discipline by telling young shoppers, "I know your mother." In 1979 a twelve-year-old boy died when a roof collapsed on him near her store, and she pushed for more Spanish-speaking firefighters.[40] After she died in 1989, La Madrina, as she was called, was inducted into the Connecticut Women's Hall of Fame, and a Frog Hollow school was named after her.

Her church was Sagrado Corazón, and the basement served as an incubator for a whole generation of Hispanic leaders—just as the rest of the neighborhood had been for industry. Sadly, in May 2017 the Archdiocese of Hartford announced the church would close as part of a sweeping plan to close twenty-six parishes after years of declining attendance and difficulties keeping older buildings up to code, among other challenges. For families who'd grown up in the church, the announcement was like a funeral.

The city's first Puerto Rican mayor, Eddie Perez, was also a former parishioner. Perez started his Hartford life as a founding member of one of the neighborhood's smaller gangs, the Ghetto Brothers, which would later merge with a larger, more dangerous group.[41] He rather quickly moved into community organizing after attending meetings in the basement of Sagrado Corazón. Perez rose to become mayor from 2001 to 2010, one of New England's first Hispanic leaders. He was also the city's first so-called strong mayor, but he left office under a cloud, on charges of accusations of bribery, fabricating evidence, and conspiracy. He recently pleaded guilty to taking a bribe and to first-degree larceny by extortion. He was given an eight-year suspended sentence and a conditional discharge, a disappointing end to the political career of a hometown-guy-made-good.

A young Eddie Perez.
Courtesy of the *Hartford
Courant*

After 1970, 45 percent of Hartford Public High's student population identified as African American, and the city became increasingly divided by race and ethnicity—African Americans to the north, and Hispanics/Latinos to the south in places like Frog Hollow. Some white residents remained in Hartford, but except for a few older families they often congregated in the western part of the city, close to the West Hartford town line.

While Hartford's Puerto Rican population was growing in influence, political power still rested in the hands of a group of longtime Hartford leaders known as the Bishops, who were mostly leaders of the local insurance and banking industry, men who served on charity boards, gave money to nonprofits, and generally steered the city in the direction they wanted it to go. The group included roughly fifteen men who met regularly for breakfast to decide the fate of the city. The relatively small size of the city made cooperation among fellows easier than in larger venues. Said one Bishop: "In New York City, you've got the downtown lower Manhattan group, and the upper Wall Street crowd. There's no other place to go in Hartford.

They bump into each other at cocktail parties, luncheons, dinners, civic affairs. . . . God, they might as well be roommates. These guys see each other daily, someplace."[42]

John Filer, former state senator who led Aetna Life & Casualty Company in the 1970s and '80s, moved to the capital city in 1958 and found that "the Chamber of Commerce had more clout than either political party, and the fabric of the city seemed relatively peaceful and unchanging. No one was protesting, the 'powerless' were so indeed, and a male, white, Anglo-Saxon Protestant was very much at home everywhere that counted."[43] Filer, the unofficial "First among Equals," was the first Bishop to encourage the group's involvement in public policy. Up to the 1970s the group had been benevolent donors, but alliances that formed with city leaders, such as city councilmember and kingmaker Nick Carbone, changed that.[44]

The group was able to wield its power with the complicity of a weak city government, led by what amounted to a figurehead mayor (elected) and a strong city manager. Ironically, the manager system of government had been endorsed in the 1940s, when the parents of the Bishops—city leaders and industry captains—worried about Hartford's loss of corporations and manufacturers moving to the suburbs.[45] The Bishops themselves would eventually be a victim of corporate mergers and moves, and longtime city residents would look back on their tenure with a mix of nostalgia and angst. The Bishops made the trains run on time, but at what cost. In a *Courant* interview in 1994, F. Peter Libassi, former Travelers senior vice president, said that the Bishops needed to be retired. "It's not the way community decisions should be made in the future," he said. "I don't condemn it for the past, but I don't think it's appropriate for the future."[46] The Bishops were no more.

At City Hall, town leaders were decrying the vast change in the city, from factories closing to residents leaving for the suburbs. It almost seemed that Hartford was in the middle of a cosmic tug-of-war.

Meanwhile, a host of homegrown neighborhood organizations were intent on improving conditions, including bringing in more affordable housing and reducing crime. One of those organizations was Hartford Areas Rally Together (HART), which focused on issues in Frog Hollow and the surrounding area. HART encouraged residents to speak up and speak out. A neighborhood newspaper, *Southside Neighborhood News*, began publishing out of HART's Park Street office. It was renamed *Hartford News* in 1987. HART staff based their work on Saul Alinsky, who according to a history of the group written in 1995, "loved to embarrass the power structure." When a landlord refused to clean up the litter around a Capitol Avenue property, the organization helped organize a dozen Babcock Street residents to protest at the West Hartford restaurant owned by the landlord.[47]

In October 1980 a group of Frog Hollow residents met with Hartford insurance officials over concerns about the potential for arson in the old buildings. Residents said seventy-five buildings in the neighborhood could be targets of "arson for profit," and every building thought to be susceptible was owned by absentee landlords. By June that year, firefighters answered calls for fifty neighborhood fires.[48] The neighborhood was suffering from not-so-benign neglect. Two years after the arson scare, homeowners protested over a merger between Connecticut Bank and Trust and Orange National Bank. The previous year, the former had granted just one five-thousand-dollar home improvement loan in the entire neighborhood, and residents had no hope that things would get better.[49] As conditions continued to deteriorate quickly, Hartford became the "perfect case-study of white flight" and the effect that flight had on the health of a city was tragic.[50] Since its peak population of 177,400 in 1950, Hartford had been steadily shrinking, with a brief swelling in the decade leading up to 1960. Most of that increase came from immigration, but once people came to Frog Hollow they often were unable to take the first step on the path to the American Dream.

In the decade between 1990 and 2000, the U.S. population increased by 13 percent. At the same time, the population of Hartford decreased by the same amount.[51] The economic and population growth of the previous century was far in the rearview mirror. Conversely, during the same period, Connecticut battled with New Jersey for the title of the state with the highest per capita income. But then Connecticut's relative high household income could be attributed largely to the incredible wealth centered on the state's Gold Coast, the part of the state that is nearest to New York City.

The rest of the state, particularly Frog Hollow, was a far different place. While people on the Gold Coast were enjoying economic success, Hartford's per capita income rarely amounted to even a third of the state's—while the income enjoyed by households in Frog Hollow was even less. In the 1990 Census, Hartford residents had the state's lowest average personal income of all Connecticut's municipalities.[52] In 1990 Connecticut's median household income was $38,870. Hartford's was $22,140. Frog Hollow's? $11,678.

Meanwhile, between 1990 and 1999, the value of taxable property in the capital city declined by 63 percent—*63 percent.* That far outstripped (by 20 percent) the average decline in other Connecticut towns, and it was especially stark compared to the uptick in the neighboring town of West Hartford, where business was (and is) booming.[53]

By the 1990s not just major manufacturing concerns were moving to the suburbs. Smaller businesses left as well. In 1993 the Bostonian Fishery, long a commercial anchor on Park Street, moved its 2,800-square-foot store to neighboring Bloomfield. The company's second-generation owner said the area's lack of parking and suburban shoppers' concerns for the safety of the neighborhood had forced the business to move out of Frog Hollow. The shop had been in Hartford since the Great Depression.[54] This too follows a familiar pattern. Suburbanites concerned about the safety of inner-city businesses stop frequenting those businesses, which means businesses must either move to where their customers are, or close. For Bostonian Fishery the move only forestalled by a few years its ultimate closure. Seven years later, the landmark building burned down on Park Street. The new Bloomfield business closed the year before that.[55]

In one study, Christian Montès, a French professor of geography and author of *American Capitals: A Historical Geography*, wrote that Hartford was in the "worst situation" with the second-highest poverty rate in the nation (30 percent). The three factors contributing to the city's downfall were, he wrote, "failing public and private leadership, disastrous racial divisions, and a home rule that favored affluent suburbs."[56]

With increasing divestment, the neighborhood became the center for dangerous gang activity, which fed into its reputation, which meant more suburbanites stayed away, which threatened more businesses, and so on. Drive-by shootings became commonplace, and when police came to collect evidence, residents who were frightened about gang retaliation kept mum.

In the early 1990s the two major gangs doing battle in Frog Hollow were the Latin Kings and Los Solidos, or the Solid Ones. The Latin Kings, with their gold and black identifying colors, started as a street gang in 1940s Chicago. One history paints the group as something of a populist uprising within the Mexican and Puerto Rican community, dedicated to fighting the "Labor Aristocracy" and a society that accused immigrants of "taking what jobs were left from the dying industrial age."[57] According to the history, the group went underground to wait for the day when members could be a part of the legitimate political process. The group was reborn in the 1960s as the Almighty Latin King Nation and would later take the name of Almighty Latin King and Queen Nation. Unfortunately, according to the history the gang learned to "use organization for capitalist purposes and the toxic biological agent known as heroin and cocaine became a player and enemy to be wary of."[58] The gang migrated to Connecticut through the prison system, where two members wrote the "King Manifesto."[59] The manifesto includes prayers for guidance and stresses that the Nation "is a religion, which gives us faith in ourselves."[60]

The group included a farm league for younger members called the Pee-Wee Kings.[61] Unlike other state- and city-based franchises within the gang system, the Connecticut Kings grew to the point that its members broke off from the original Chicago organization, and the Hartford Kings set up shop in crumbling Frog Hollow.

The Connecticut prison system also served as a farm system for Los Solidos, which formed in the early 1990s after the consolidation of two other gangs—Savage Nomads and Ghetto Brothers (former mayor Eddie Perez's old gang)—whose members were bent on rivalry with the larger, better-organized Kings.[62] As with the Kings, Los Solidos, known more commonly as "Solids," offered both a family and a business structure. Unlike the Kings, the Solids' rulebook contained little about spirituality. In April 1995 *Harper's Magazine* published the secret rulebook of Los Solidos Nation, which included admonitions about punishment such as "termination, beat down, or even death."[63] The structure was decidedly capitalistic. From the rulebook: "As a Nation of Solid Brothers, our plans for the future are to have a chain of stores, have Brothers as lawyers, doctors and politicians, and have our families be well-off. But we have to start slowly and climb this ladder of success and fortune gradually."[64]

Ironically, though the stock-in-trade was prostitution and drugs, the rulebook said: "The family and friends you grew up with are now addicted to drugs. Don't turn your back on them. Look out for them, put them in rehab, and give them a reason to better themselves. . . . The majority of young males in our communities today don't have any family. That's why they're out running around and acting all crazy and foolish. But if you give them an opportunity to be part of

Marble walls defaced in Hartford Superior Court, Morgan Street. Red enamel and black spray paint. April 25, 1981. Courtesy of the *Hartford Courant*

Hartford police question suspected Latin Kings about the shooting of a man who died from his wounds. June 9, 1993. Photo by Cecilia Préstamo. Courtesy of the *Hartford Courant*

Robert Sorenson, director of St. Elizabeth House, accepts a check donation from Latin Kings and Los Solidos families. Check for $400 will go toward the soup kitchen at the center. June 22, 1993. Photo by Cecilia Préstamo. Courtesy of the *Hartford Courant*

a family, they will always be grateful to you and look up to you. They will be the kind of Brothers who will always be loyal to you and to the Family."[65]

Albert DiChiara, of the University of Hartford's department of sociology and criminal justice, studied Los Solidos and came away with a more nuanced view of the organization and its structure and purpose. According to DiChiara, in the early 1990s the Solids "considered itself a political organization, albeit one that saw fit to use criminal activities to further the interests of its members."[66] Crime and political activity coexisted in these "really emergent social formations that must continually respond to a variety of situational challenges and social forces."[67] That nuance was lost on most Frog Hollow residents. Alta Lash, executive director of the nonprofit United Connecticut Action for Neighborhoods and a longtime resident of Frog Hollow, remembers the day the gangs took over her block. It was a spring day in 1990 and neighbors were in their yards, tending gardens and chatting over fences. A group of young men went from door to door announcing that they now ruled the neighborhood. Some families simply left their homes and never came back. Two left with their front doors standing open, Lash said. As with other economically vulnerable residents, Lash couldn't afford to move and so she hunkered down to ride out what amounted to an occupation.[68]

Then-mayor Carrie Saxon Perry held a meeting in 1992 and asked, frustrated, if a particular street in Hartford needed to be renamed Latin Kings Boulevard, for all the gang activity that went on there. The city had the feel of a village under siege. A task force to address gang violence intermittently stemmed the tide, but then there'd be more gunshots.

In 1992 officials launched Operation Liberty with state and federal support. The initiative involved the kind of aggressive police action

Former Hartford mayor Carrie Saxon Perry. Courtesy of the *Hartford Courant*

that has gained so much attention in other cities—though the ACLU of Connecticut heard no complaints at the time.[69] Cars were stopped and searched. Streets were targeted for surveillance. Results were immediate. In the first few weeks, officers stopped two thousand cars and made two hundred arrests that included seventy-five suspected gang members. This was out of some three hundred suspected Hartford members of the Los Solidos and twenty-five hundred Kings statewide.[70]

Gang members were not immune to public relations, and some of them made efforts at it. In May 1993 Los Solidos members participated in a Frog Hollow street cleanup. Community organizers feared violence when the Latin Kings said they'd show up too. On the other hand, according to a stunning *Hartford Courant* story written by Mary Otto, organizers thought the turf war might abate when gang members saw how rundown the blocks had become. Why would they fight over garbage-strewn streets? The gangs showed up in their respective colors—red and blue for the Solids, gold and black for the Kings. Prior to the pickup, a tiny French Canadian woman lectured the children gathered in the basement of St. Anne's Church: "Everything gonna be copacetic." And it was.

But that was just one public relations move in a sea of bullets and beatdowns. Connecticut's location between the urban centers of Boston and New York puts its neighborhoods directly in line between the two cities' drug trade. By some estimates, gang members were responsible for 35 percent of the city's drug offenses and 15 percent of property crimes. (City activists said the figures were probably low.) Bullets were flying all over Frog Hollow. Teenagers with no gang affiliation were shot. An old woman sweeping her porch on Zion Street, shot.

And then a shy little seven-year-old girl was shot in her family's car, and the tide began to turn. On March 26, 1994, a member of Los Solidos had been taken and held by the Latin Kings in an apartment in Charter Oak Terrace, just south of Frog Hollow. That night the Delgado family, including Angel and his wife, Maria, and their three daughters, climbed into a borrowed gray Toyota, which Angel, a mechanic, had just repaired. They drove from their Park Street apartment to drop off milk at the kids' grandmother's house in nearby Charter Oak. As they sat parked at the curb at the older woman's house, a red Camaro pulled alongside. In later court testimony, Maria Delgado described how the car was less than two feet away when someone opened fire. Solidos members had mistaken the borrowed car for that of a rival member of the Latin Kings. One bullet hit Angel Delgado in the stomach. Another hit the Delgado's middle daughter, Marcelina, in the head. She died three days later.

Classmates at Parkville Community School planted a tree in her honor. Signs in Marcelina's memory dotted Frog Hollow businesses. Random violence was one thing. This violence had a name on it, and that name was Marcelina's.

Through concerted efforts from the federal to the local level, seven members of Los Solidos were found and charged with the killing of the girl. Two years after her death, the city's police chief, Joseph Croughwell, said the mood in the city was "a complete 180 from when Marcelina was killed."[71] The drug kingpin who had ordered the shooting was eventually sentenced to thirteen life terms in prison. The increased police effort—as well as stories of some notable gang members publicly leaving the life—decreased the violence in the neighborhood immeasurably. It hasn't gone away, not by half, but gang activity is not nearly as violent and unpredictable as it was in the 1990s. The blatant activity that once took over Frog Hollow's streets has been replaced by quieter, smaller groups more interested in making money from drugs than showing their colors.

But how many young men and women of color were locked up for their gang and drug activities in what the *Courant* called a "lost generation?" And how many remain behind bars, caught in the net of failed public policy that brought aggressive police activity to a neighborhood that would have benefited more from jobs? The War on Drugs caused massive collateral damage in urban neighborhoods such as Frog Hollow.[72] As David Simon and Edward Burns wrote in their 2013 *The Corner: A Year in the Life of an Inner-City Neighborhood*, on which an Emmy-winning HBO miniseries is based, "In Baltimore, not only is the street-level drug arrest not a solution, it's actually part of the problem." The same held true in Hartford. When former president Barack Obama tried to change the language around the so-called war, he did so with the understanding that words guide public policy, and not always in a good way.[73]

The recent history of the neighborhood was never just about crime and gangs. While the Solids and Kings were attempting hostile takeovers of one another, businesses opened on Park Street. Employees at Aetna volunteered their lunch hours to read to children at Burns School. Neighborhood groups continued to provide a stable backbone and backstop for Frog Hollow residents. Neighborhood parents decided their children needed a safe place to play and organized the construction of a five-million-dollar community center in Pope Park.[74]

In 1998 neighbors in north Frog Hollow complained to Hartford Areas Rally Together that their insurance rates had jumped, though statewide insurance rates had dropped. Property owners said that insurance was being pushed out of their financial reach. That meant there was little incentive to repair or even keep up a building. A *Courant* editorial opined, "It would be ironic if an inability to get insurance hastened the demise of a neighborhood in the Insurance City."[75]

In 2003 the Travelers Property Casualty Corporation and the St. Paul Companies merged and announced that the headquarters would leave Hartford for Minneapolis, which prompted the *New York Times* to trumpet that Hartford, long the center of the insurance industry, was now ceding the title. "There will still be plenty of insurance-business jobs in Hartford. But what the shift means to the culture of a place that traditionally looked to the giants of the insurance industry for leadership is less clear," said the *Times*.[76]

It seemed that the only thing that slowed white flight was the relative lack of remaining white families who could flee. Most had already left. Through it all, the neighborhood's Park Street has remained a vibrant business center. It is the Hispanic cultural center for southern New England, yet Frog Hollow remains one of Hartford's poorest zip codes. A recent U.S. Census says the annual income for nearly 60 percent of Frog Hollow's households is less than $25,000. By comparison the average household income in Connecticut hovers around $64,000. Here are some other numbers:

The median Frog Hollow household income, averaging the three census tracts that make up the neighborhood, is $28,529, while the median household income in the rest of Hartford is $32,095. Compare that to Connecticut, where the median income is $71,755.

Over 79 percent of children in Frog Hollow live in single-parent households, and 90 percent of those are headed by single mothers. Among those single parents, nearly half are not in the workforce. A recent UnitedHealthcare study, "America's Health Rankings," says the child poverty rate in Connecticut is 12.3 percent, compared to 41.3 percent in Hartford. In Frog Hollow, the child poverty rate is nearly 58 percent.

At 16 percent, Frog Hollow has the highest unemployment rate in the state. This statistic does not include individuals who have stopped looking for work or who are part of a steady influx of new arrivals who have not yet begun to search. Information from the most recent U.S. Census says that within Frog Hollow, 50 percent of males over sixteen and 61 percent of females over sixteen are not in the workforce.

Frog Hollow was never a wealthy neighborhood, but for the past 160-plus years it served as a springboard from which immigrants could bounce to the suburbs. John Gregory Dunne said in a 1977 interview with the *Washington Post* that though he had lived in many places, he appreciated most his childhood in Frog Hollow, where he watched his Grandfather Burns, the Pope of Park Street, work his magic with the other new immigrants. John Gregory Dunne was fond of saying that his family rose from "steerage to suburbia in three generations." And isn't that what we expect from the American Dream?

The city and state has felt the effect of a reduction in defense spending that for generations contributed to the state's economic well-being. Between 1964 and 1987, 21 percent of the state's manufacturing base was in defense-related industries. That meant 86,000 jobs.[77] The majority of defense employees worked in the aircraft and parts industry. During that same time period, manufacturing shrunk at the rate of 1 percent a year, while employment in aircraft and ship production grew.[78]

By 2013, with military spending shrinking even more, the defense industry accounted for roughly 50,000 jobs, or 10 percent of the state's economy, according to Bob Ross, executive director of the state's office of military affairs, a state entity that serves as a liaison between the government/defense industry and military families.[79] (A recent proposed budget from the Trump administration called for a $54 billion increase in defense spending, but that proposal may have come too late for neighborhoods like Frog Hollow. Many of the factories are gone, turned to housing or fallen deeply into decrepitude.)

The decline in military spending in a way mirrors the decline of manufacturing in Frog Hollow, though decline in the latter could differ by a factor of one hundred. For decades, Frog Hollow *was* manufacturing, and when it no longer was manufacturing it became one big hole that needed filling.

The neighborhood continued to shift. In 2000 the Immaculate

Conception Church—where the Pope of Park Street once donated a pew and where generations of immigrating Catholics were given entrée into the culture of Frog Hollow and beyond—merged with St. Anne's down the street. The homeless shelter started by Father Donagher in the basement had grown and St. Anne's, which had catered to French Canadians (and later French- and Creole-speaking Haitians), needed the parishioners.[80] Lawrence/Burns School became the Dominick F. Burns Latino Studies Academy. At the rededication in 2013, members of Burns's family listened to students speak about dreams that included, "I have a dream that Burns won't be known as the school with the lowest test scores."[81]

Cindy Martinez grew up in the Clay-Arsenal neighborhood of Hartford, in the central-northern part of the city. Though the area had a rough reputation, Martinez remembers a neighborhood where residents went Christmas caroling—sometimes one hundred at a time—and a well-stocked library was just two blocks from her house. Yes, there was gang activity, but Martinez remembers gang members

Cindy Martinez.
Courtesy of Cindy Martinez

who let children know when to clear the streets in advance of coming violence.

Martinez didn't realize her family was poor until her tenth birthday when she came upon her parents counting money on the table, only to come up too short for buying her a cake. "My dad would work extra hours and do whatever it took to make sure we had a nice dining room table, nice couches, and make sure we had nice things so we would never question we were poor," she said. That tenth birthday was only a temporary disappointment because Martinez's father hit the lottery and the family won $250.

When she was in high school, her parents split up and she moved with her mother to Frog Hollow, to an apartment on the corner of Putnam and Rusk, across from Burns School. At the time, the neighborhood was at the tail end of a vicious drug war pitting the Latin Kings against Los Solidos. Martinez worried that with her then-spotty Spanish she wouldn't be Puerto Rican enough for her new street, that she would be labeled a "boot-leg Puerto Rican." And her reputation was important, she said, because the hollow was solidly Puerto Rican. People dressed, she was told, like they'd just stepped off the island. If she looked too Americanized, she said, "they were going to smell it immediately." This was a common concern. Martinez's parents had migrated from Puerto Rico when they were both children. Concerned about the education their children might (not) receive in Hartford schools, they had their children bypass bilingual classes, a step Martinez regrets now.

"We would have been so much farther ahead," she said. Even today, she said, "I speak Spanish," but not as well as she'd like to.

Martinez found refuge at the Greater Hartford Academy of the Arts, located on the sixteen-acre Learning Corridor near Trinity College. There she saw a production from HartBeat Ensemble, a provocative theater group founded in 2001 that has explored such topics as human trafficking and bullying and that stages an annual

Hartford take on *A Christmas Carol*. At a production attended by Martinez, one of the actors pretended to not want to get onstage. The audience erupted, but Martinez sensed it was part of the show. Afterward, she went to HartBeat cofounder Julia B. Rosenblatt to compliment her.

"Don't listen to them," she told Rosenblatt. "That was pretty bad-ass."

Later, when the theater needed an intern, Rosenblatt tracked down Martinez, who never left. Recently the theater started a Neighborhood Investigative Project that is looking, one by one, at the city's neighborhoods. Martinez wrote and codirected "Frog Hollow, a State of Mind" after months of interviews of both longtime residents and recent immigrants. Her characters included Lion Lady and her son, Princey-Boy, who navigate the streets of the neighborhood. The characters are restless, openhearted, and anxious to embrace their past and run headlong into the future. In that, they are Frog Hollow. Right up until opening night, Martinez worried whether the production would do justice to her neighborhood. How do you portray a neighborhood so rich in history and so diverse in makeup?

"I needed to feel that I did right by the neighborhood," said Martinez. She said that in the Latino community there was progress, and people who wanted progress, even when there was an "us versus them" mentality. "There have always been these waves crashing."

9. Regardless of Fortuitous Circumstances

THE GHOSTS THAT WALK FROG HOLLOW'S
STREETS, AND WHERE THEY'RE HEADING

Drive the streets of Frog Hollow. Drive down Capitol Avenue and notice the compact, block-long brick building at the corner of Flower Street, where mixed-income apartments will fill what was once Pratt & Whitney's factory. Swing down Columbia Avenue and look at the former company housing. Head down Babcock—named for the newspaper owner—and check out the Perfect Sixes and their porches and their small yards whose boundaries are marked by knee-high wrought-iron fences.

Ghosts walk these streets, the ghosts of the Babcocks, of ham-fisted Isaac Kroopneck, and Maria Sánchez, La Madrina, who made the city of Hartford her family. The shades of tiny newspaper vendors stand on the corners and shout over one another. The ghosts of bars long closed hold their customers, who emerge from dank cells to hand a coin to the vendors, and stumble home to families of four, five, and six in cold-water flats they feel fortunate to have.

Ghost whistles call workers to their stations. Ghost children skip down streets bearing metal lunch buckets for their ghost fathers, who will enjoy a homemade meal, fresh from the stove; or, at Pope Manufacturing, they'll walk to the clean, bright lunchroom and pay a few bits for a sumptuous meal. On weekends ghost families sit in pews and listen to priests decry the evils of Sunday baseball, but they sneak out early to sit with large woven baskets on gently sloping hills—God's own bleachers—to watch what will become America's pastime. Ghost car horns honk, urging children off of Park Street and into the cool air of the corner library. All ghosts. All gone.

But not really.

There is still, despite time and the river washing through the streets and yards of Frog Hollow, a certain feel, a vibe, an All-American sense of can-do. If all evidence is to the contrary, the hope of the American Dream lives scattered among yesterday's ghosts and today's well-kept gardens and iffy cars your neighbor will fix for cheap.

Hartford, with a population of 125,000, has shrunk every decade since 1950, when the population peaked at 177,000. It is known as an "inelastic" city. An elastic city embraces and encourages housing, shopping, and industry within its borders. An inelastic city allows residents to escape to its neighboring towns where tax bases benefit from the extra bodies. Inelastic cities sit surrounded by suburbs with public services and schools that make the urban schools and public services look shabby by comparison.[1] Inelastic cities lean toward extreme racial segregation, with an insufficient tax base and a heavy reliance on state and federal aid that is subject to the political winds.[2]

Kansas City, Mo., is an elastic city.[3] Hartford is not. One writer said Hartford is on life support, but Hartford's obituary has been written and rewritten too many times to count.[4] So have Detroit's and Newark's, because each city has been created as their "own suburbs' poorhouses."[5] It is as if this is what we wanted, these abandoned neighborhoods in struggling cities. If it's not what we wanted, it is certainly what we planned for. We did this. We created the Frog Hollows of Connecticut and elsewhere by neglect—benign and enforced—and now we act as if we're at a loss as to what to do. So we continue doing nothing, which allows us to continue to complain.

At a 2016 mayor's forum on affordable housing hosted by the Connecticut Mortgage Bankers Association, three town leaders—mayors from Hartford and New London, as well as the first selectman from Stonington—agreed that the lack of regional planning in the state is hurting cities. This is a conversation that has gone on for decades. Hartford and the rest of Connecticut are 169 fiefdoms with moats dug around them. That means, save for the scattered regional school districts, that each town has its own school board, its own emergency response system, its own fleet of snow plows. This is an expensive exclusivity. So long as "regionalism" remains a dirty word in Connecticut, Hartford will continue to struggle.

But there are signs of life. The old Billings & Spencer tool factory was acquired by the Melville Charitable Trust in 2005 as a cornerstone of the Billings Forge Community Works initiative. The trust is the country's largest antihomelessness foundation, and today approximately 270 residents live in Billings Forge's ninety-eight units of mixed-income affordable housing. Amenities include a community center and computer lab, an on-site laundry facility, on-site property management, kitchens with all major appliances, hardwood floors, large bay windows, and oversized closets, among other things.

Other signs of life: though some neighbors oppose it, the old Lyric Theatre at Broad and Park is supposed to be torn down to make way for an expanded Park Street branch of the library, which as one of the state's most active library branches is bursting at the seams at a rented building on Park and Babcock. (Neighbors who oppose the destruction want the building to be preserved, though decades of neglect may have made that impossible.[6]) And that could be a metaphor for the rest of Frog Hollow: decades of neglect have turned the blocks into something unfixable. Yet there is opportunity for development of other buildings in the neighborhood, and sometimes it takes an outsider to notice it. In 2003 Jane Holtz Kay, architect and design critic for the *Nation* and author of *Asphalt Nation*, wrote a guest column for the *Courant* and quoted from an earlier *New York Times* article that called Hartford the "most destitute 17 square miles in the nation's wealthiest state." Instead of destitution, she suggested critics look at the Learning Corridor, which Trinity College's then-president, Evan Dobelle, started in 1996 with help from people like Eddie Perez. Kay called the Corridor "novel and workable." In an earlier essay, Dobelle wrote that the Corridor "will be a model for the country." He also wrote, "This project had to succeed because the people in our neighborhood had had their hopes dashed too many times."

And sometimes it takes an insider to notice. The children of Mi Casa Family Services and Educational Center, in a book published in 2015 about homelessness in their community, suggest taking the multiple abandoned buildings they walk by every day and turning them into homes with kitchens and bedrooms and doors that shut. And why not?

First, you have to believe. Kicking Hartford is a perverted kind of pastime for some, particularly for people who don't live there. It's great fun (for some) to throw rocks over the town line about Hartford's politics, about Hartford's schools, about a baseball stadium that stalled downtown—though once it opened, it drew in some of the largest crowds of its league. Why does that get lost?

A recent survey by WalletHub.org ranked Hartford forty-ninth in a list of best state capitals. Only Jackson, Miss., scored lower.[7] That story got more traction than it deserved. Read the online comments in the *Hartford Courant*. They are notoriously negative about the capital city, and that shows a shocking lack of understanding of what it takes to make a state healthy. The capital city is the beating heart of the state. If the heart isn't vibrant, the state doesn't have a chance. Those half-baked criticisms miss the point.

The city of Hartford doubles in size every workday. Eighty-three percent of the town's 121,000 jobs are held by commuters, while 65 percent of Hartford residents leave the city for their work.[8] Of the Hartford workers who commute out, a whopping 75 percent make less than $40,000 a year. Hartford is a cheap place to live, nestled in the eighth-most expensive state for housing. A National Low Income Housing Coalition report from 2017 said the housing wage of an average state resident—or the amount of money a person must earn per hour to afford a decent two-bedroom home—is $24.72. The state's minimum wage is $10.10. At that rate, the average minimum wage earner in Connecticut must work ninety-eight hours a week just to afford a two-bedroom place to live. Never mind food and health care.

Frog Hollow has an indoor plaza, El Mercado, with some of the best Dominican food around. There are also Peruvian and Colombian restaurants, surrounded by Mexican and Honduran businesses, all within a stone's throw of one another. The neighborhood is home to one of the state's more active library branches, on Park Street. When the Cotto family ran it, Frog Hollow was also home to La Paloma Sabanera, a funky coffee shop that gained national attention for its stubborn belief in the city. La Paloma was one of those vaunted "third places" first noted by Ray Oldenburg for their ability to bring people together in a public—though oddly private—setting. Having such a space, wrote Oldenburg, is vital to democracy and to the well-being of those living in it.[9] At La Paloma, the great and the lowly came together over coffee and poetry. One of its owners, Luis Cotto, was elected to the Hartford Court of Common Council on the Working Families ticket. He left that position and is now executive director of Egleston Square Main Street, dedicated to promoting the area between Roxbury and Jamaica Plain in Boston. He, in a word, bounced. In 2015 the family's coffee shop was replaced by Little River Restoratives, an upscale restaurant named for the river than once ran through the neighborhood. Celebrating yet another anniversary, it is defying the odds, once again.

In the last, bruising presidential election there was much conversation—at least from one presidential candidate—about taking America back to a mythical time of greatness, to a time when, it must be said, the power rested in the hands of a few, mostly white, brokers. Frog Hollow, for all its bumps and bruises, is a vital and living place, where the churn of new immigrants keeps things fresh. If America will be great, it will be great because of places like Frog Hollow, where families—and not just white ones—have the opportunity to start over. They get a little wiggle room to learn the lingo, the lay of the land. And then they bounce.

In that spirit of the place, earlier neighborhood residents—the Babcocks, the Beechers, the Kroopnecks—would have felt very much at home. Neighborhoods like Frog Hollow can still be laboratories for innovation and nurseries for the American Dream. We may not agree on what it is, but we can't quite retire the notion of an American Dream. It's as good as in our DNA. Along with Hartford, it has been given its last rites multiple times, but the American Dream is never far from our conversations.

Yet the Dream has always been offered with conditions. *If* you work hard. *If* you keep your head down. Recent events and social movements such as Occupy Wall Street and Black Lives Matter have reminded us that piled atop one another, those ifs will eventually crush us. *If* you're born white. *If* you're born male. *If* you're born in a certain zip code, then that will be a bigger determinant of your health than your genetic code.

If we stop there, we will be left with a master's class on how to kill a once-vibrant neighborhood and an ongoing dream:

Segregate the residents by race and class.

Make it easy—attractive, even—for businesses to move to the suburbs.

Divest as much as legally possible (and in some cases more, if you can get away with it) from neighborhood schools, emergency services, and other infrastructure that define a town and make a neighborhood healthy.

Then sit back and listen to the death rattle as a neighborhood breathes its last.

But this is Hartford, a town that despite the worst efforts of people who should know better, keeps on breathing. And this is Frog Hollow. Neither will go quietly.

In the end, we return to James Truslow Adams and that damn American Dream. Can someone still start from nothing, and through hard work and good luck Make It? Through its history, Frog Hollow has been a place to test that theory, from the *American Mercury*, a newspaper that survived when others did not; to innovative indus-trialists anxious to mine the latest research and create a future; to generations of families who took a chance by moving to the city. Recent residents are no different, but there must be an understanding of policies and strategies that, intended or otherwise, divested untold wealth from the neighborhood and left it to survive on its own. If we do not name these policies and strategies, we haven't a hope of learning from them.

Frog Hollow's residents have always been ready for the next big thing, and I look forward to that because that too is part of the Dream—death, renewal, transformation, and then change. Second chances. And third. And sometimes fourth. Entities that aren't often seen together, but in Frog Hollow, they just fit. The Hindu flags flut-tering on Broad Street next to a car dealership next to public housing next to a corner food market. Frog Hollow has survived flood and flux, abject poverty, a booming economy, and long, hot baseball games. It has been messy and sometimes hopeless, and still the heart of the neighborhood is beating, and with it—yes!—the American Dream.

Acknowledgments

A book may be written in a vacuum (or at least it feels that way) but it is not published in one. Thank you to the wonderful Suzanna Tamminen, Wesleyan University Press director and editor in chief; and the inestimable Susan Abel, University Press of New England production editor, and Jeffrey Wyneken, who painstakingly copyedited every word of this manuscript. I have to say, after working closely with Jeff, I'm a little nervous about this thank-you, because Jeff won't have edited it. I hope I got it right.

Notes

Introduction

1. James Truslow Adams, *The Epic of America* (New York: Blue Ribbon Books, 1931), 214–15.

2. James Truslow Adams, *The Epic of America* (Piscataway, N.J.: Transaction, 2012), x.

3. Mark Roberts, Thomas A. Hirschi, and Kirk A. Foster, *Chasing the American Dream: Understanding What Shapes Our Fortunes* (New York: Oxford University Press, 2014), 42.

1. The Difficult Dream

1. Mariano Hernandez, *The Ultimate Guide to Architecture* (Raleigh, N.C.: Lulu Press, 2015), 1918.

2. John Frederick Kelly, *The Early Domestic Architecture of Connecticut* (North Chelmsford, Mass.: Courier Corporation, 1924), 2.

3. Kevin Murphy, *Water for Hartford: The Story of the Hartford Water Works and the Metropolitan District Commission* (Middletown, Conn.: Wesleyan University Press, 2010), 9.

4. Ibid.

5. John Treadwell, Enoch Perkins, and Thomas Day, *Public Statute Laws [of] the [State of] Connecticut, Part 1* (Hartford, Conn.: Hudson and Goodwin, 1808), 46.

6. "Babcock's Well," *Hartford Daily Courant* (1840–87), July 12, 1847, 2. http://search.proquest.com/docview/552823925?_accountid=46995.

7. Murphy, *Water for Hartford*, 9.

8. Richard Joseph Purcell, *Connecticut in Transition, 1775–1818* (Hartford, Conn.: American Historical Association, 1918), 421.

9. Charles Burr Todd, *Life and Letters of Joel Barlow, LL.D., Poet, Statesman, Philosopher, with Extracts from His Works and Hitherto Unpublished Poems* (New York: G. P. Putnam's Sons, 1886), 47.

10. John Bard McNulty, *Older Than the Nation: The Story of the Hartford Courant* (Stonington, Conn.: Pequot Press, 1964), 15.

11. Martin Schultz and Herman R. Lantz, "Occupational Pursuits of Free Women in Early America: An Examination of Eighteenth-Century Newspapers," *Sociological Forum* 3, no. 1 (1988): 89–109. www.jstor.org/stable/684623.

12. Lawrence H. Leder, "The Role of Newspapers in Early America 'In Defense of Their Own Liberty,'" *Huntington Library Quarterly* 30, no. 1 (1966): 1–16, 15. doi: 10.2307/3816757.

13. Phillip I. Blumberg, *Repressive Jurisprudence in the Early American Republic: The First Amendment and the Legacy of English Law* (Cambridge, U.K.: Cambridge University Press, 2010), 218.

14. "A Look Backward," *Hartford Daily Courant* (1840–87), April 30, 1883, 2. http://search.proquest.com/docview/554185478?_accountid=46995.

15. www.cthistoryonline.org/cdm/singleitem/collection/cho/id/17033/rec/6, retrieved July 12, 2015.

16. John P. Kaminski and Richard Leffler, "Religion in the Early Republic," Federal Judicial Center, 11. http://csac.history.wisc.edu/religion_in_the_early_republic.pdf, retrieved March 17, 2017.

17. Larry E. Tise, *The American Counterrevolution: A Retreat from Liberty, 1783–1800* (Mechanicsburg, Penn.: Stackpole Books, 1998), 389.

18. Eric D. Lehman and Amy Nawrocki, *Literary Connecticut: The Hartford Wits, Mark Twain, and the New Millennium* (Charleston, S.C.: History Press, 2014), 30.

19. Darrel Abel, *The Nascence of American Literature* (Bloomington, Ind.: iUniverse, 2002), 225.

20. Joe Nunes, "Chapter One: With Thanks to Benjamin Franklin," *Hartford Courant*, October 18, 2014. www.courant.com/courant-250/your-moments/hc-courant-chapter-one-20141018-story.html.

21. A. J. Valente, *Rag Paper Manufacture in the United States, 1801–1900* (Jefferson, N.C.: McFarland, 2010), 8.

22. John Bidwell, *American Paper Mills, 1690–1832: A Dictionary of the Paper Trade, with Notes on Products, Watermarks, Distribution Methods, and Manufacturing Techniques* (Lebanon, N.H.: University Press of New England, 2013), 176.

23. Peter P. Hill, *Joel Barlow: American Diplomat and Nation Builder* (Dulles, Va.: Potomac Books, 2012), 3.

24. Richard R. John, *Spreading the News: The American Postal System from Franklin to Morse* (Cambridge, Mass.: Harvard University Press, 2009), 25.

25. Stephen L. Vaughn, *Encyclopedia of American Journalism* (New York: Routledge, 2007), 399.

26. John, *Spreading the News*, 37.

27. Paul Starr, *The Creation of the Media: Political Origins of Modern Communications* (New York: Basic Books, 2005), 90.

28. "From the American Mercury of April 1, 1817," *Connecticut Courant* (1791–1837), April 8, 1817, 3. http://search.proquest.com/docview /548550838?_accountid=46995.

29. Richard Buel Jr., *Joel Barlow: American Citizen in a Revolutionary World* (Baltimore: Johns Hopkins University Press, 2011), 69.

30. Royal Ralph Hinman, *A Catalogue of the Names of the Early Puritan Settlers of the Colony of Connecticut: With the Time of Their Arrival in the Country and Colony, Their Standing in Society, Place of Residence, Condition in Life, Where from, Business, &C, As Far As Is Found on Record* (Hartford, Conn.: Case, Tiffany, 1852), 94.

31. Susan E. Klepp, *Revolutionary Conceptions: Women, Fertility, and Family Limitation in America, 1760–1820* (Chapel Hill: University of North Carolina Press, 2009), 4.

32. Klepp, *Revolutionary Conceptions*, 6.

33. "Classified Ad 3—No Title," *Connecticut Courant* (1791–1837), May 26, 1818, 1. http://search.proquest.com/docview/552446976?_account id=46995.

34. "Classified Ad 2—No Title," *Connecticut Courant* (1791–1837), May 12, 1818, 3. http://search.proquest.com/docview/552453369?_account id=46995.

35. "Brief Mention," *Hartford Daily Courant* (1840–1887), December 29, 1871, 2. http://search.proquest.com/docview/553749110?_accountid=46995.

36. "Front Page 2—No Title," *Hartford Daily Courant* (1840–1887), October 4, 1877, 1. http://search.proquest.com/docview/554031246?_accountid=46995.

37. Bernard L. Herman, *Town House: Architecture and Material Life in the Early American City, 1780–1830* (Chapel Hill: University of North Carolina Press, 2012), 96.

38. Acts and Laws of the State of Connecticut (1820), 432.

39. Connecticut Historical Society, "Gilman Family Papers." https://chs.org/finding_aides/finding_aids/gilmf1787.html, retrieved June 13, 2016.

2. *An Opportunity for Each*

1. "First Commercial Telephone Exchange—Today in History: Jan. 28." http://connecticuthistory.org/the-first-commercial-telephone-exchange-today-in-history/, retrieved January 13, 2017.

2. "Inventing Entertainment: The Early Motion Pictures and Sound Recordings of the Edison Companies," Library of Congress. www.loc.gov/collections/edison-company-motion-pictures-and-sound-recordings/articles-and-essays/history-of-edison-sound-recordings/history-of-the-cylinder-phonograph/, retrieved January 13, 2017.

3. Richard Knowles Morris, *John P. Holland, 1841–1914, Inventor of the Modern Submarine* (Annapolis, Md.: United States Naval Institute, 1966), 175.

4. Peter George, *The Emergence of Industrial America: Strategic Factors in American Economic Growth since 1870* (Albany: State University of New York Press, 2012), 138.

5. Bruce D. Epperson, *Peddling Bicycles to America: The Rise of an Industry* (Jefferson, N.C.: McFarland, 2010), 30.

6. David Hounshell, *From the American System to Mass Production, 1800–1932: The Development of Manufacturing in the United States* (Baltimore: Johns Hopkins University Press, 1985), 194.

7. Joseph F. Healey, *Diversity and Society: Race, Ethnicity, and Gender* (New York: SAGE, 2013), 132.

8. *The Iron Age*, vol. 75 (Southborough, Mass., 1905), 1053.

9. "Manufacturing Notes," *Hartford Daily Courant* (1840–87), April 3, 1878, 1. http://search.proquest.com/docview/554037974?_accountid =46995.

10. Epperson, *Peddling Bicycles to America*, 29.

11. George, *Emergence of Industrial America*, 138.

12. Healey, *Diversity and Society*, 132.

13. "The Hartford Machine Screw Company," *Hartford Daily Courant* (1840–87), March 9, 1880, 2. http://search.proquest.com/docview /554122365?_accountid=46995.

14. Harlan Lane, *When the Mind Hears: A History of the Deaf* (New York: Knopf Doubleday, 2010), 442.

15. Timothy E. Scheurer, *Born in the U.S.A.: The Myth of America in Popular Music from Colonial Times to the Present* (Jackson: University Press of Mississippi, 2007), 49.

16. William DeLoss Love, *The Colonial History of Hartford: Gathered from the Original Records* (self-published, 1914), 196.

17. Love, *Colonial History of Hartford*, 196.

18. Stephen Innes, *Labor in a New Land: Economy and Society in Seventeenth-Century Springfield* (Princeton, N.J.: Princeton University Press, 2014), 82.

19. Christopher G. Bates, *The Early Republic and Antebellum America: An Encyclopedia of Social, Political, Cultural, and Economic History* (New York: Routledge, 2015), 1069.

20. James Hammond Trumbull, *The Memorial History of Hartford County, Connecticut, 1633–1884*, vol. 1 (Hartford, Conn.: E. L. Osgood, 1886), 372.

21. Love, *Colonial History of Hartford*, 115.

22. Ibid., 196.

23. *Publications of the Municipal Art Society of Hartford, Connecticut, Bulletin*, no. 809 (1908): 23.

24. F. Perry Close, *History of Hartford Streets: Their Origin and Dates of Use* (Hartford: Connecticut Historical Society, 1969).

25. John Walter, *Rifles of the World* (Iola, Wis.: JP Media, 2006), 437.

26. Ellsworth Grant, "The Miracle on Capital Ave.," *Hog River Journal* (May–July 2004): 25.

27. Debby Applegate, *The Most Famous Man in America* (New York: Doubleday, 2006), 282.

28. "City Intelligence," *Hartford Daily Courant* (1840–77), January 23, 1864, 2. http://search.proquest.com/docview/552645631?_accountid =46995.

29. Hounshell, *From the American System to Mass Production,*194.

30. *Commemorative Biographical Record of Hartford County, Conn.: Containing Biographical Sketches of Prominent and Representative Citizens, and of Many of the Early Settled Families,* vol. 1 (Hartford, Conn.: J. H. Beers & Co., 1901), 234.

31. www.nytimes.com/1864/12/16/news/weed-sewing-machine.html, retrieved April 2, 2017.

32. "Enlarging Business—The Weed Sewing Machine," *Hartford Daily Courant* (1840–87), August 29, 1865, 2. http://search.proquest.com/doc view/553447318?_accountid=46995.

33. Hounshell, *From the American System to Mass Production,*193.

34. Arthur P. Molella and Anna Karvellas, *Places of Invention* (Washington, D.C.: Smithsonian Institution, 2015), 108.

35. "The Weed Sewing Machine Company—Opening of the Hartford Office," *Hartford Daily Courant* (1840–87), May 1, 1866, 2. http://search .proquest.com/docview/553512144?_accountid=46995.

36. "Something New," *Hartford Daily Courant* (1840–87), November 16, 1866, 8. http://search.proquest.com/docview/553521412?_accountid=46995.

37. *The Great Trial, or Contest between Sewing Machines under the Direction of the Maryland Institute, Baltimore, Md.* (Hartford, Conn.: Hutchings Printing House, 1869), 22.

38. *New York Times,* December 16, 1864. https://search-proquest-com .unh-proxy01.newhaven.edu/hnpnewyorktimes/docview/91839862/360F 047DACE431APQ/1?accountid=8117.

39. "The Weed Sewing Machine Company," *Hartford Daily Courant* (1840–87), September 25, 1871, 2. http://search.proquest.com/docview /553745213?_accountid=46995.

40. Russell Conwell, "Acres of Diamonds." www.americanrhetoric.com /speeches/rconwellacresofdiamonds.htm, retrieved October 16, 2015.

41. Joseph E. Gortych, *Consider a Spherical Patent: IPR and Patenting in Technological Business* (Boca Raton, Fla.: CRC Press, 2014), 209.

42. Charles Louis Flint, Charles Frances McCay, John Clark Merriam, Thomas Prentice Kettell, and Linus Pierpont Brockett, *One Hundred Years' Progress of the United States* (Hartford, Conn.: L. Stebbins Publishing, 1871), 429.

43. Ibid., 428.

44. "The Weed Sewing Machine Factory," *Hartford Daily Courant* (1840–87), September 25, 1866, 8. http://search.proquest.com/docview /553503785?_accountid=46995.

45. "The Weed Sewing Machine Company," *Hartford Daily Courant* (1840–87), August 3, 1865, 2. http://search.proquest.com/docview /553495578?_accountid=46995.

46. "The Weed Sewing Machine at Vienna," *Hartford Daily Courant* (1840–87), September 16, 1873, 2. http://search.proquest.com/docview /553784821?_accountid=46995.

47. *Red Bluff Independent*, no. 11, September 27, 1873, 4, Advertisements, Column 2.

48. Smithsonian Trade Literature Collection. www.sil.si.edu/ DigitalCollections/Trade-Literature/Sewing-Machines/NMAHTEX /0606/imagepages/image1.htm, retrieved October 16, 2015.

49. "Hartford's Great Fire," *Hartford Courant* (1887–1922), February 14, 1894, 6. http://search.proquest.com/docview/194100496?_accountid =46995.

50. "Burning of Colt's Armory," *Hartford Daily Courant* (1840–87), February 6, 1864, 2. http://search.proquest.com/docview/552646532? _accountid=46995.

51. "Colt Armory Burns—Today in History: February 4." http:// connecticuthistory.org/colt-armory-burns-today-in-history/, retrieved March 16, 2016.

52. Molella and Karvellas, *Places of Invention*, 103.

53. Ibid., 97.

54. "A Big 'Deal,'" *Hartford Courant* (1887–1922), April 21, 1890, 1. http://search.proquest.com/docview/554415135?_accountid=46995.

55. Correspondence of the *Courant*, "Deserted New England Farms," *Hartford Courant* (1887–1922), January 27, 1892, 6. http://search.proquest.com/docview/554471382?_accountid=46995.

56. "When It's Made in Hartford, It's Made Right," *Hartford Courant* (1887–1922), February 19, 1912, 2-xi. http://search.proquest.com/docview/555878506?_accountid=46995.

57. Molella and Karvellas, *Places of Invention*, 122.

58. Mark Twain, *What Is Man and Other Essays*. https://ebooks.adelaide.edu.au/t/twain/mark/what_is_man/index.html, retrieved January 14, 2017.

59. Hounshell, *From the American System to Mass Production*, 203.

60. Ibid., 194.

61. "Export of Bicycles," *Hartford Courant* (1887–1922), October 24, 1899, 5. http://search.proquest.com/docview/554891687?_accountid=46995.

62. Grant, "Miracle on Capital Ave.," 25.

63. Stephen B. Goddard, *Colonel Albert Pope and His American Dream Machines: The Life and Times of a Bicycle* (Jefferson, N.C.: McFarland, 2000), 110.

64. Glen Norcliffe, *Critical Geographies of Cycling: History, Political Economy and Culture* (Burlington, Vt.: Ashgate, 2015), 89.

65. Ibid., 92.

66. "The Famous 'Columbia' Bicycle," *The National Magazine*, vol. 17, 1893, 392.

67. "Will Return to Work," *Hartford Courant* (1887–1922), June 1, 1901, 1. http://search.proquest.com/docview/554995524?_accountid=46995.

68. John Alexpoulos, *The Nineteenth Century Parks of Hartford* (Hartford, Conn.: Hartford Architecture Conservancy, 1982), 25.

69. Richard DeLuca, "The League of American Wheelmen and Hartford's Albert Pope Champion the Good Roads Movement." http://connecticuthistory.org/the-league-of-american-wheelmen-and-the-good-roads-movement-how-popes-bicycles-led-to-good-roads/, retrieved June 1, 2016.

70. William Greenleaf, *Monopoly on Wheels: Henry Ford and the Selden Automobile Patent* (Detroit: Wayne State University Press, 2011), 60.

71. Bernard C. Beaudreau, *Mass Production, the Stock Market Crash, and the Great Depression: The Macroeconomics of Electrification* (Bloomington, Ind.: iUniverse, 2004), 3.

72. Goddard, *Colonel Albert Pope and His American Dream Machines*, 217.

73. Greenleaf, *Monopoly on Wheels*, 62.

74. Vincent Curcio, *Henry Ford* (Oxford, U.K.: Oxford University Press, 2013), 24.

75. Ibid.

76. "Columbia Cars, Forecast for 1906," *Hartford Courant* (1887–1922), October 3, 1905, 4. http://search.proquest.com/docview/555332201?_accountid=46995.

77. "Sharps Rifle Company," *Hartford Daily Courant* (1840–87), June 1, 1875. http://search.proquest.com/docview/553880769?_accountind_46995.

78. "Weed Sewing Machine Company," *Hartford Daily Courant* (1840–87), February 5, 1886, 3. http://search.proquest.com/docview/554259823?_accountid=46995.

79. "Billings-Spencer Become Owners of Columbia Factory," *Hartford Courant* (1887–1922), July 1, 1914, 6. http://search.proquest.com/docview/556126450?_accountid=46995.

80. "What Bank Means to Park Street," *Hartford Courant* (1887–1922), October 25, 1919. http://search.proquest.com/docview/556740306?_accountid=46995.

81. Katherine Johns-Galvin, "A Green Oasis in a Food Desert: Increasing the Accessibility of Affordable Healthy Foods in an Urban Neighborhood in Hartford, CT" (master's thesis, Central Connecticut State University, 2011), 7.

82. David Drury, *Hartford in World War I* (Mount Pleasant, S.C.: Arcadia, 2015), 33.

83. "Hundreds of Hartford Women Do War Work in Local Factories," *Hartford Courant* (1887–1922), December 2, 1917, 1. http://search.proquest.com/docview/556543699?_accountid=46995.

84. D. D. Bidwell, "Vast Expansion in Hartford during War May Be Matched by Great Prosperity of Peace," *Hartford Courant* (1887–1922), June 29, 1919. http://search.proquest.com/docview/556697871?_accountid =46995.

85. "Snow in October," *Hartford Courant* (1887–1922), October 13, 1917, 10. http://search.proquest.com/docview/556513804?_accountid=46995.

86. "Coal Shortage Is 50,000,000 Tons," *Hartford Courant* (1887–1922), November 15, 1917, 12. http://search.proquest.com/docview/556518391? _accountid=46995.

87. Hamilton Cravens, *Great Depression: People and Perspectives* (Santa Barbara, Calif.: ABC-CLIO, 2009), 7.

88. S. Paul Garner, "Application of Burden in Wartime Industries," *Southern Economic Journal* 11, no. 4 (1945): 360–68, 361. doi: 10.2307/1053372.

89. Ann R. Markusen, *The Rise of the Gunbelt: The Military Remapping of Industrial America* (Cambridge, U.K.: Oxford University Press, 1991), 131.

90. David Radcliffe, *Charter Oak Terrace: Life, Death and Rebirth of a Public Housing Project* (Hartford, Conn.: Southside Media, 1998), 2.

91. Peter Townsend, *Pear Harbor Jazz: Changes in Popular Music in the Early 1940s* (Jackson: University Press of Mississippi, 2009), 23.

92. "World War II." http://connecticuthistory.org/topics-page/world -war-ii/, retrieved March 18, 2016.

93. "The Travelers Corporation." www.encyclopedia.com/doc/1G2 -2840700137.html, retrieved April 25, 2016.

94. "Accident Insurance," *Hartford Daily Courant* (1840–87), December 15, 1869, 2. http://search.proquest.com/docview/553628068?_accountid =46995.

95. William Howe Tolman, *Social Engineering: A Record of Things Done by American Industrialists Employing Upwards of One and One-Half Million of People* (New York: McGraw Publishing, 1909), 119.

96. Ibid., 120.

97. "Mitchell on Industrial Accidents," *Hartford Courant* (1887–1922), March 23, 1911, 8. http://search.proquest.com/docview/555793387? _accountid=46995.

98. "Editorial Article 3—No Title," *Hartford Courant* (1887–1922), April 30, 1910, 8. http://search.proquest.com/docview/555712371?_accountid =46995.

99. "100 Workmen Are Dying Each Day," *Hartford Courant* (1887–1922), February 24, 1912, 9. http://search.proquest.com/docview/555876047? _accountid=46995.

100. Ibid.

101. Ibid.

102. "Social Movement Is Making a Change," *Hartford Courant* (1887–1922), February 18, 1911, 14. http://search.proquest.com/docview /555790697?_accountid=46995.

103. Jonathan Levy, *Freaks of Fortune: The Emerging World of Capitalism and Risk in America* (Cambridge, Mass.: Harvard University Press, 2012), 174.

104. "Accident Insurance History Is Traced," *Hartford Courant* (1887– 1922), February 18, 1922, 12. http://search.proquest.com/docview /557030277?_accountid=46995.

105. Robin Pearson and Takau Yoneyama, *Corporate Forms and Organisational Choice in International Insurance* (Cambridge, U.K.: Oxford University Press, 2015), 141.

3. A Dream of Social Order

1. Epperson, *Peddling Bicycles to America*, 155.

2. Norcliffe, *Critical Geographies of Cycling*, 94.

3. "This House Home of Presidents," *Hartford Courant* (1887–1922), January 8, 1906, 3. http://search.proquest.com/docview/555352666? _accountid=46995.

4. Trumbull, *Memorial History of Hartford County*, 379.

5. J. A. T., "The Asphalt Pavement," *Hartford Courant* (1887–1922), January 15, 1901. http://search.proquest.com/docview/554977544? _accountid=46995.

6. "What It Means to Be a Hartford Traffic Policeman," *Hartford Courant* (1887–1922), August 8, 1915. http://search.proquest.com/doc view/556261883?_accountid=46995.

7. Alexis C. Madrigal, "The Racist Housing Policy That Made Your Neighborhood," *Atlantic*, May 22, 2014. www.theatlantic.com/business/archive/2014/05/the-racist-housing-policy-that-made-your-neighborhood/371439/.

8. Hartford's Trinity College has done some extraordinary research on this, available at http://ontheline.trincoll.edu/book/.

9. Peter Wallison, *Hidden in Plain Sight: What Really Caused the World's Worst Financial Crisis and Why It Could Happen Again* (New York: Encounter Books, 2015), 101.

10. Shaun McGann and Jack Dougherty, "Federal Lending and Redlining." http://epress.trincoll.edu/ontheline2015/chapter/federal-lending-and-redlining/, retrieved March 22, 2016.

11. David Goldfield, *Encyclopedia of American Urban History* (New York: SAGE, 2006), 531.

12. Shawn McGann, "The Effects of 'Redlining' on the Hartford Metropolitan Region." http://connecticuthistory.org/the-effects-of-redlining-on-the-hartford-metropolitan-region/, retrieved March 22, 2016.

13. See http://salt.umd.edu/T-RACES/collaborate.html.

14. "Form 8, 10–1–37, Area Description—Security Map of Hartford, HOLC." http://magic.lib.uconn.edu/magic_2/vector/37840/primary_source/hdimg_37840_064_1937_holc_national_archives_trinity_grade_c8.pdf, retrieved March 22, 2016.

15. Mary Daly, "Race Restrictive Covenants in Property Deeds." http://connecticuthistory.org/race-restrictive-covenants-in-property-deeds/, retrieved March 22, 2016.

16. James W. Loewen, *Sundown Towns: A Hidden Dimension of American Racism* (New York: New Press, 2013), 129.

17. Ibid.

18. Ibid.

19. Marc Settles, "Racial Segregation in America: Historical Discrimination, Modern Forms of Exclusion, and Inclusionary Remedies," *Journal of Land Use and Environmental Law* (1996). http://archive.law.fsu.edu/journals/landuse/Vol141/seit.htm?referer=www.clickfind.com.au, retrieved April 2, 2016.

20. Nancy O. Albert, "A Tale of Two Cities: The Rise and Fall of Public Housing," *Hog River Journal*, www.hogriver.org/issues/v01n02/two_cities .htm, retrieved March 30, 2016.

21. John Atlas and Peter Dreier, "Public Housing: What Went Wrong?" *Shelterforce Online*, no. 74 (September/October 1994). www.nhi.org/online /issues/77/pubhsg.html.

22. Lawrence M. Friedman, "Public Housing and the Poor: An Overview," *California Law Review* 54, no. 2 (1966): 643. http://scholarship.law .berkeley.edu/cgi/viewcontent.cgi?_article=2930&context=californialaw review.

23. Alexander von Hoffman, "History Lessons for Today's Housing Policy: The Political Processes of Making Low-Income Housing Policy," Joint Center for Housing Studies, Harvard University, August 2012, 1. www.jchs .harvard.edu/sites/jchs.harvard.edu/files/w12–5_von_hoffman.pdf.

24. Ibid., 2.

25. Atlas and Dreier, "Public Housing."

26. "Housing Yearbook 1942," National Association of Housing Officials. https://archive.org/stream/housingyearbook42natirich/housingyear book42natirich_djvu.txt, retrieved April 1, 2016.

27. Emily Meehan, "The Debate over Who Could Occupy World War II Public Housing in West Hartford." http://connecticuthistory.org/the -debate-over-who-could-occupy-world-war-ii-public-housing-in-west -hartford/, retrieved April 1, 2016.

28. Ibid.

29. Frank Andrews Stone, *African American Connecticut: The Black Scene in a New England State: Eighteenth to Twenty-First Century* (Bloomington, Ind.: Trafford, 2008), 216.

30. Richard H. Foster, "Wartime Trailer Housing in the San Francisco Bay Area," *Geographical Review* 70, no. 3 (1980): 276–90, 276. doi: 10.2307/214256.

31. Jill Suzanne Shook, *Making Housing Happen, Faith-Based Affordable Housing* (Eugene, Ore.: Wipf and Stock, 2012), 23.

32. Catherine Bauer, "The Dreary Deadlock of Public Housing," *Architectural Forum* (May 1957): 140. http://isites.harvard.edu/fs/docs/icb

.topic753413.files/20% 20Public% 20Housing% 20in% 20Europe% 20and% 20America% 20% 20Nov% 2012/Catherine% 20Bauer% 20Deadlock.pdf, retrieved March 31, 2016.

33. *Report of the Inter-Racial Commission.* Digest of Connecticut Administrative Reports to the Governor, vol. 4, 1949–50, 8.

34. Robert Fishman, *Bourgeois Utopias: The Rise and Fall of Suburbia* (New York: Basic Books, 2008), 21.

35. Joseph F. DiMento, "Stent (or Dagger?) in the Heart of Town: Urban Freeways in Syracuse, 1944–1967," Legal Studies Research Paper, no. 2009–16, University of California, Irvine, School of Law. http://poseidon01.ssrn.com/delivery.php, retrieved March 18, 2016.

36. *Interstate 50: 50 Years of the Dwight D. Eisenhower National System of Interstate and Defense Highways* (Tampa, Fla.: Faircount, 2006), 16.

37. Gregg Mangan, *On This Day in Connecticut History* (Mount Pleasant, S.C.: Arcadia, 2015), 288.

38. Daniel T. Lichter and Glenn V. Fuguitt, "Demographic Response to Transportation Innovation: The Case of the Interstate Highway," *Social Forces* 59, no. 2 (1980): 492–512, 493. doi: 10.2307/2578033.

39. Alana Semuels, "The Role of Highways in American Poverty," *Atlantic,* www.theatlantic.com/business/archive/2016/03/role-of-highways-in-american-poverty/474282/? utm_source=SFTwitter, retrieved March 18, 2016.

40. Elsa Nunez, *Hanging Out and Hanging On: From the Projects to the Campus* (New York: Rowman & Littlefield, 2014), 31.

41. "Metro Hartford Progress Points 2014." www.metrohartfordprogresspoints.org/downloads/Metro_Hartford_Progress_Points_2014.pdf, retrieved May 28, 2016.

42. Kenneth J. Neubeck and Richard E. Ratcliff, "Urban Democracy and the Power of Corporate Capital: Struggles over Downtown Growth and Neighborhood Strategies in Hartford, Connecticut," in *Business Elites and Urban Development: Case Studies and Critical Perspectives,* edited by Scott Cummings (Albany: State University of New York Press, 1988), 299.

43. Adam Podgorecki, Jon Alexander, and Rob Shields, *Social Engineering* (Montreal: McGill-Queen's Press, 1996), 1.

44. José Cruz, *Identity and Power: Puerto Rican Politics and the Challenge of Ethnicity* (Philadelphia: Temple University Press, 2010), 102.

45. Tom Condon, "Visionary '70s Plan Reimagined Region," *Hartford Courant*, March 13, 2011. http://search.proquest.com/docview/857636992 ?_accountid=46995.

46. Cruz, *Identity and Power*, 102.

47. Norman Krumholz and Pierre Clavel, *Reinventing Cities: Equity Planners Tell Their Stories* (Philadelphia: Temple University Press, 1994), 174.

48. Cruz, *Identity and Power*, 103.

49. Andrew Walsh, "Hartford: A Global History," in *Confronting Urban Legacy: Rediscovering Hartford and New England's Forgotten Cities*, edited by Xiangming Chen and Nick Bacon (London: Lexington Books, 2013), 101. Italics mine.

50. Ibid.

51. "Travelers Official to Retire in 1993," *Hartford Courant*, September 9, 1992, F3. http://search.proquest.com/docview/255305442?_accountid =46995.

52. Michael Paul Sacks, "Suburbanization and Racial/Ethnic Divide in the Hartford Metropolitan Area," August 2003, 5. http://digitalrepository .trincoll.edu/cgi/viewcontent.cgi?_article=1016&context=hartford_papers.

53. Radcliffe, *Charter Oak Terrace*.

54. Albert Chevan, "The Growth of Home Ownership: 1940–1980," *Demography* 26, no. 2 (1989): 249–66, 249. www.jstor.org/stable/2061523.

55. Peter Dreier, "Reagan's Legacy: Homelessness in America," *Shelterforce Online*, no. 135 (May/June 2004). http://nhi.org/online/issues/135 /reagan.html.

56. Padraig O'Malley, *Homelessness: New England and Beyond* (Amherst: University of Massachusetts Press, 1992), 654.

57. John M. Murrin, Paul E. Johnson, James M. McPherson, Alice Fahs, and Gary Gerstle, *Liberty, Equality and Power: A History of the American People* (Boston: Cengage Learning, 2007), 880.

58. Lisa Pierce Flores, *The History of Puerto Rico* (Santa Barbara, Calif.: ABC-CLIO, 2009), 101.

59. Susan Campbell, "Sal Moves In, Highlighting Connecticut's Uneven Record on Housing," WNPR, May 18, 2015. http://wnpr.org/post/sal-moves-highlighting-connecticuts-uneven-record-housing-needy#stream/0.

60. O'Malley, *Homelessness*, 703.

61. U.S. Census American FactFinder: https://factfinder.census.gov/faces/tableservices/jsf/pages/productview.xhtml?src=bkmk.

4. The Fullest Stature

1. "20 Hartford Widows Would Benefit by State Pension Fund," *Hartford Courant* (1887–1922), August 6, 1919, 3. http://search.proquest.com/docview/556729669?_accountid=46995.

2. Ron Welburn, *Hartford's Ann Plato and the Native Borders of Identity* (Albany: State University of New York Press, 2015), 50.

3. Lucianne Levin, *Connecticut's Indigenous Peoples: What Archaeology, History and Oral Tradition Teach Us about Their Communities and Cultures* (New Haven, Conn.: Yale University Press, 2013), 200.

4. Joseph Olcott Goodwin, *East Hartford: Its History and Traditions* (East Hartford, Conn.: Case, 1879), 28.

5. Charles F. Johnson, "The Dutch in Hartford," in *Hartford in History: A Series of Papers by Resident Authors*, edited by Willis I. Twitchell (Hartford, Conn.: Plimpton, 1899). http://theancientburyingground.org/the-dutch-in-hartford/, retrieved 10/20/15.

6. Ibid.

7. Wick Griswold, *A History of the Connecticut River* (Charleston, S.C.: History Press, 2012), 33.

8. Roxanne Dunbar-Ortiz, *An Indigenous Peoples' History of the United States* (Boston: Beacon Press, 2015), 18.

9. Wilson H. Faude, *Hidden History of Connecticut* (Mount Pleasant, S.C.: History Press, 2010), 9.

10. Helen Ainslie Smith, *The Thirteen Colonies: New Jersey, Delaware, Maryland, Pennsylvania, Connecticut, Rhode Island, North Carolina, South Carolina, Georgia* (New York: G. P. Putnam's Sons, 1901), 245.

11. John William De Forest, *History of the Indians of Connecticut from the Earliest Known Period to 1850* (self-published, 1853), 83.

12. Brad D. Lookingfill, *American Military History: A Documentary Reader* (Hoboken, N.J.: John Wiley, 2010), 9.

13. "The 'Praying Towns,'" Nipmuc Indian Association of Connecticut, Historical Series no. 2, 2nd ed., 1995. www.nativetech.org/Nipmuc/praytown.html.

14. Christos G. Frentzos and Antonio S. Thompson, *The Routledge Handbook of American Military and Diplomatic History: The Colonial Period to 1877* (London: Routledge, 2014), 27.

15. Alfred A. Cave, *The Pequot War* (Amherst: University of Massachusetts Press, 1996), 151.

16. Paul Finkelman, *Encyclopedia of African-American History, 1619–1845: From the Colonial Period to the Age of Frederick Douglass* (London: Oxford University Press, 2006), 33.

17. William Henry Gocher, *Wadsworth: Or, the Charter Oak* (Hartford, Conn.: W. H. Gocher, 1904), 125.

18. The Chiel Amang, Y. E., "Reminiscences and Studies," *Hartford Daily Courant* (1840–87), March 7, 1873, 2. http://search.proquest.com/docview/553781122?_accountid=46995.

19. Gocher, *Wadsworth*, 104.

20. "Charter Oak," *Hartford Daily Courant* (1840–87), August 22, 1866, 8. http://search.proquest.com/docview/553529080?_accountid=46995.

21. Gocher, *Wadsworth*, 124.

22. De Forest, *History of the Indians of Connecticut*, 72.

23. *Original Distribution of the Lands among the Settlers, 1639* (Hartford, Conn.: Connecticut Historical Society, 1912), vii.

24. Ibid.

25. C., "Hartford," *Hartford Daily Courant* (1840–87), January 28, 1852, 2. http://search.proquest.com/docview/552953976?_accountid=46995.

26. S. Scott Rohrer, *Wandering Souls: Protestant Migrations in America, 1630–1865* (Chapel Hill: University of North Carolina Press, 2010), 35.

27. *Hartford District, 1635–1700* (Baltimore: Genealogical Publishing Co., 1904), 239.

28. Love, *Colonial History of Hartford*, 135.

29. Trumbull, *Memorial History of Hartford County*, 221.

30. John Duffy, *The Sanitarians: A History of American Public Health* (Champaign: University of Illinois Press, 1992), 12.

31. "United States of America," World Health Organization. www.who .int/substance_abuse/publications/global_alcohol_report/profiles/usa .pdf, retrieved March 26, 2016.

32. Corin Hirsch, *Forgotten Drinks of Colonial New England: From Flips and Rattle-Skulls to Switchel and Spruce Beer* (Gloucestershire, U.K.: History Press, 2014), 20.

33. Trumbull, *Memorial History of Hartford County*, 350.

34. Amy Mittelman, *Brewing Battles: A History of American Beer* (New York: Algora, 2008), 9.

35. Edwin Pond Parker, *History of the Second Church of Christ in Hartford* (Hartford, Conn.: Belknap & Warfield, 1892), 16.

36. Frederick Clifton Pierce, *Field Genealogy: Being the Record of All the Field Family in America* (Chicago: W. B. Conkey Co., 1901), 339.

37. *The Cyclopaedia of Temperance and Prohibition: A Reference Book of Facts, Statistics, and General Information of All Phases of the Drink Question, the Temperance Movement, and the Prohibition Agitation* (New York: Funk & Wagnalls, 1891), 416.

38. S. H. Riddel, "Temperance Circular," *Connecticut Courant* (1791–1837), November 24, 1834, 3. http://search.proquest.com/docview /548546742?_accountid=46995.

39. Daniel Okrent, *Last Call: The Rise and Fall of Prohibition* (New York: Simon & Schuster, 2010), 12.

40. Louis Filler, *The Crusade against Slavery* (Piscataway, N.J.: Transaction, 1960), 41.

41. Henry Stephen Clubb, *Results of Prohibition in Connecticut, Being Special Returns Retrieved from Every County As to the Effects of the Maine Liquor Law* (Hartford, Conn.: Flowers & Company, 1855), 99.

42. "Prohibition in Hartford," *Hartford Daily Courant* (1840–87), March 8, 1855, 2. http://search.proquest.com/docview/553109166?_accountid=46995.

43. John Newton Stearns, *Prohibition Does Prohibit, Or, Prohibition Not a Failure* (New York: National Temperance Society & Publication House, 1875), 24.

44. *Cyclopaedia of Temperance and Prohibition*, 127.

45. Stearns, *Prohibition Does Prohibit*, 25.

46. Walter W. Scott, ed., *A Handbook for the Aggressive Temperance People of the United States*, rarebooksclub.com, 2012, 43.

47. Okrent, *Last Call*, 105.

48. Albert Edward Van Dusen, *Connecticut* (New York: Random House, 1961), 282.

49. Deets Pickett, Clarence True Wilson, and Ernest Dailey Smith, *The Cyclopedia of Temperance, Prohibition and Morals* (New York: Methodist Book Concern, 1917), 59.

50. *American Prohibition Year Book* (Lincoln Temperance Press, 1908), 44. https://books.google.com/books.

51. "City Health Department Credits Prohibition for Decrease in Death Rate," *Hartford Courant* (1887–1922), November 28, 1920, 1. http://search .proquest.com/docview/556864730?_accountid=46995.

52. "Drunks Jailed Prove Prohibition Failure, Say County Officials," *Hartford Courant* (1887–1922), December 3, 1920, 10. http://search .proquest.com/docview/556882263?_accountid=46995.

53. "Unintended Consequences," pbs.org, 2011. www.pbs.org/kenburns /prohibition/unintended-consequences/.

54. "Prohibition Failure in City of Hartford, Police Board Agrees," *Hartford Courant* (1887–1922), November 14, 1922. http://search.proquest .com/docview/557126871?_accountid=46995.

55. Karen M. Hess, Christine Hess Orthmann, and Henry Lim Cho, *Introduction to Law Enforcement and Criminal Justice* (Boston: Cengage Learning, 2014), 30.

56. Lisa McGirr, *The War on Alcohol: Prohibition and the Rise of the American State* (New York: W. W. Norton, 2015), xix.

57. Michael Newton, *The Encyclopedia of Serial Killers* (New York: Facts on File, 2006), 4.

58. Municipal Register of the City of Hartford, October 28, 1918, 460.

59. Will Siss, *Connecticut Beer: A History of Nutmeg State Brewing* (Mount Pleasant, S.C.: Arcadia, 2015), 21–22.

60. Mike Messina, "Diamonds of the Past: Hartford's Lost Ball Parks." http://connecticuthistory.org/diamonds-of-the-past-hartfords-lost-ball -parks/, retrieved March 20, 2016.

61. "To Start Factory League," *Hartford Courant* (1887–1922), June 2, 1904, 2. http://search.proquest.com/docview/555228659?_accountid =46995.

62. "Factory League," *Hartford Courant* (1887–1922), May 17, 1905, 2. http://search.proquest.com/docview/555300567?_accountid=46995.

63. "A Plea for Quiet," *Hartford Courant* (1887–1922), August 5, 1901, 7. http://search.proquest.com/docview/555085268?_accountid=46995.

64. "No Sunday Baseball," *Hartford Courant* (1887–1922), August 19, 1901, 7. http://search.proquest.com/docview/555001954?_accountid =46995.

65. "Sunday Baseball," *Hartford Courant* (1887–1922), August 10, 1901, 4. http://search.proquest.com/docview/555081279?_accountid=46995.

66. "Sporting Gossip," *Hartford Courant* (1887–1922), October 6, 1908, 13. http://search.proquest.com/docview/555584810?_accountid=46995.

67. "Tiger Cadets Play a Tie," *Hartford Courant* (1887–1922), November 1, 1909, 10. http://search.proquest.com/docview/555677595?_accountid =46995.

68. Jack Dwyer, "Letter from Carlisles," *Hartford Courant* (1887–1922), October 10, 1912, 16. http://search.proquest.com/docview/555943843? _accountid=46995.

69. "Rev. R. B. Ogilby Is Named to Succeed Dr. Flavel S. Luther," *Hartford Courant* (1887–1922), April 25, 1920, 1. http://search.proquest .com/docview/556797775?_accountid=46995.

70. "All Frog Hollow Gives Rousing Reception to Its Idol, 'Spud' Drew," *Hartford Courant* (1887–1922), November 18, 1920, 16. http://search .proquest.com/docview/556866153?_accountid=46995.

71. David R. Woodward, *World War I Almanac* (New York: Infobase, 2009), 232.

72. "Russell Gives Directions for Saving Coal," *Hartford Courant* (1887–1922), October 8, 1918, 5. http://search.proquest.com/docview/556616961?_accountid=46995.

73. "Furnaces in Discard," *Hartford Courant* (1887–1922), January 27, 1918, 11. http://search.proquest.com/docview/556541150?_accountid=46995.

74. Maurine Weiner Greenwald, *Women, War, and Work: The Impact of World War I on Women Workers in the United States* (Ithaca, N.Y.: Cornell University Press, 1990), Preface.

75. "1920 Eventful Period in History of Connecticut's Capital City," *Hartford Courant* (1887–1922), December 31, 1920, 10. http://search.proquest.com/docview/556872039?_accountid=46995.

76. Cravens, *Great Depression*, 56.

77. Peter Tuckel, Kurt Schlichting, and Richard Maisel, "Social, Economic, and Residential Diversity within Hartford's African American Community at the Beginning of the Great Migration," *Journal of Black Studies* 37, no. 5 (May 2007): 715.

78. Robert Haws, *The Age of Segregation: Race Relations in the South, 1890–1945* (Jackson: University Press of Mississippi, 1978), 92.

79. Sarajane Cedrone, "Southern Blacks Transform Connecticut." http://ctexplored.org/southern-blacks-transform-connecticut/, retrieved April 10, 2016.

80. Roger Bruns, *Martin Luther King, Jr.: A Biography* (Santa Barbara, Calif.: Greenwood, 2006), 10.

81. Stone, *African American Connecticut*, 217.

82. Philip J. Wood, *Southern Capitalism: The Political Economy of North Carolina, 1880–1980* (Durham, N.C.: Duke University Press, 1976), 174.

83. Jim Powell, "How Did Rich Connecticut Morph into One of America's Worst-Performing Economies?" *Forbes*, August 1, 2013. www.forbes.com/sites/jimpowell/2013/08/01/how-did-rich-connecticut-morph-into-one-of-americas-worst-performing-economies/#1416f471270e.

84. Carolyn C. Jones, "Split Income and Separate Spheres: Tax Law and Gender Roles in the 1940s," *Law and History Review* 6, no. 2 (1988): 259–310, 263. doi: 10.2307/743685.

85. Maureen Honey, *Creating Rosie the Riveter: Class, Gender, and*

Propaganda during World War II (Amherst: University of Massachusetts Press, 1985), 176.

86. Jones, "Split Income and Separate Spheres," 264.

87. Sherrie A. Kossoudji and Laura J. Dresser, "Working Class Rosies: Women Industrial Workers during World War II," *Journal of Economic History* 52, no. 2 (1992): 431–46, 432. www.jstor.org/stable/2123119.

88. Sara Harrington, "Women's Work: Domestic Labor in American World War II Posters," *Art Documentation: Journal of the Art Libraries Society of North America* 22, no. 2 (2003): 41–44, 43. www.jstor.org/stable /27949264.

89. Jones, "Split Income and Separate Spheres," 263.

90. "Women in Industry," *Monthly Labor Review* 57, no. 4 (1943): 723–28, 723. www.jstor.org/stable/41817253.

91. Martin H. Blatt and Martha K. Norkunas, *Work, Recreation, and Culture: Essays in American Labor History* (New York: Routledge, 2013), 13.

92. Susan E. Riley, "Caring for Rosie's Children: Federal Child Care Policies in the World War II Era," *Polity* 26, no. 4 (1994): 655–75, 656. doi: 10.2307/3235099.

93. Claudia D. Goldin, "The Role of World War II in the Rise of Women's Employment," *American Economic Review* 8, no. 4 (1991): 741–56, 741. www.jstor.org/stable/2006640.

94. Doris Weatherford, *American Women during World War II* (New York: Routledge, 2009), 405.

95. Valerie K. Oppenheimer, "The Interaction of Demand and Supply and Its Effect on the Female Labour Force in the United States," *Population Studies* 21, no. 3 (1967): 239–59, 239. doi: 10.2307/2173145.

96. Ibid.

5. To Be Recognized

1. "20 Hartford Widows Would Benefit by State Pension Fund," *Hartford Courant* (1887–1922), August 6, 1919, 3. http://search.proquest.com /docview/556729669?_accountid=46995.

2. Ron Welburn, *Hartford's Ann Plato and the Native Borders of Identity* (Albany: State University of New York Press, 2015), 50.

3. Lucianne Levin, *Connecticut's Indigenous Peoples: What Archaeology, History and Oral Tradition Teach Us about Their Communities and Cultures* (New Haven, Conn.: Yale University Press, 2013), 200.

4. Joseph Olcott Goodwin, *East Hartford: Its History and Traditions* (East Hartford, Conn.: Case, 1879), 28.

5. Charles F. Johnson, "The Dutch in Hartford," in *Hartford in History: A Series of Papers by Resident Authors*, edited by Willis I. Twitchell (Hartford, Conn.: Plimpton, 1899). http://theancientburyingground.org /the-dutch-in-hartford/, retrieved 10/20/15.

6. Ibid.

7. Wick Griswold, *A History of the Connecticut River* (Charleston, S.C.: History Press, 2012), 33.

8. Roxanne Dunbar-Ortiz, *An Indigenous Peoples' History of the United States* (Boston: Beacon Press, 2015), 18.

9. Wilson H. Faude, *Hidden History of Connecticut* (Mount Pleasant, S.C.: History Press, 2010), 9.

10. Helen Ainslie Smith, *The Thirteen Colonies: New Jersey, Delaware, Maryland, Pennsylvania, Connecticut, Rhode Island, North Carolina, South Carolina, Georgia* (New York: G. P. Putnam's Sons, 1901), 245.

11. John William De Forest, *History of the Indians of Connecticut from the Earliest Known Period to 1850* (self-published, 1853), 83.

12. Brad D. Lookingfill, *American Military History: A Documentary Reader* (Hoboken, N.J.: John Wiley, 2010), 9.

13. "The 'Praying Towns,'" Nipmuc Indian Association of Connecticut, Historical Series no. 2, 2nd ed., 1995. www.nativetech.org/Nipmuc/pray town.html.

14. Christos G. Frentzos and Antonio S. Thompson, *The Routledge Handbook of American Military and Diplomatic History: The Colonial Period to 1877* (London: Routledge, 2014), 27.

15. Alfred A. Cave, *The Pequot War* (Amherst: University of Massachusetts Press, 1996), 151.

16. Paul Finkelman, *Encyclopedia of African-American History, 1619–1845: From the Colonial Period to the Age of Frederick Douglass* (London: Oxford University Press, 2006), 33.

17. William Henry Gocher, *Wadsworth: Or, the Charter Oak* (Hartford, Conn.: W. H. Gocher, 1904), 125.

18. The Chiel Amang, Y. E., "Reminiscences and Studies," *Hartford Daily Courant* (1840–87), March 7, 1873, 2. http://search.proquest.com/docview /553781122?_accountid=46995.

19. Gocher, *Wadsworth*, 104.

20. "Charter Oak," *Hartford Daily Courant* (1840–87), August 22, 1866, 8. http://search.proquest.com/docview/553529080?_accountid=46995.

21. Gocher, *Wadsworth*, 124.

22. De Forest, *History of the Indians of Connecticut*, 72.

23. *Original Distribution of the Lands among the Settlers, 1639* (Hartford, Conn.: Connecticut Historical Society, 1912), vii.

24. Ibid.

25. C., "Hartford," *Hartford Daily Courant* (1840–87), January 28, 1852, 2. http://search.proquest.com/docview/552953976?_accountid=46995.

26. S. Scott Rohrer, *Wandering Souls: Protestant Migrations in America, 1630–1865* (Chapel Hill: University of North Carolina Press, 2010), 35.

27. *Hartford District, 1635–1700* (Baltimore: Genealogical Publishing Co., 1904), 239.

28. Love, *Colonial History of Hartford*, 135.

29. Trumbull, *Memorial History of Hartford County*, 221.

30. John Duffy, *The Sanitarians: A History of American Public Health* (Champaign: University of Illinois Press, 1992), 12.

31. "United States of America," World Health Organization. www.who. int/substance_abuse/publications/global_alcohol_report/profiles/usa.pdf, retrieved March 26, 2016.

32. Corin Hirsch, *Forgotten Drinks of Colonial New England: From Flips and Rattle-Skulls to Switchel and Spruce Beer* (Gloucestershire, U.K.: History Press, 2014), 20.

33. Trumbull, *Memorial History of Hartford County*, 350.

34. Amy Mittelman, *Brewing Battles: A History of American Beer* (New York: Algora, 2008), 9.

35. Edwin Pond Parker, *History of the Second Church of Christ in Hartford* (Hartford, Conn.: Belknap & Warfield, 1892), 16.

36. Frederick Clifton Pierce, *Field Genealogy: Being the Record of All the Field Family in America* (Chicago: W. B. Conkey Co., 1901), 339.

37. *The Cyclopaedia of Temperance and Prohibition: A Reference Book of Facts, Statistics, and General Information of All Phases of the Drink Question, the Temperance Movement, and the Prohibition Agitation* (New York: Funk & Wagnalls, 1891), 416.

38. S. H. Riddel, "Temperance Circular," *Connecticut Courant* (1791–1837), November 24, 1834, 3. http://search.proquest.com/docview/548546742?_accountid=46995.

39. Daniel Okrent, *Last Call: The Rise and Fall of Prohibition* (New York: Simon & Schuster, 2010), 12.

40. Louis Filler, *The Crusade against Slavery* (Piscataway, N.J.: Transaction, 1960), 41.

41. Henry Stephen Clubb, *Results of Prohibition in Connecticut, Being Special Returns Retrieved from Every County As to the Effects of the Maine Liquor Law* (Hartford, Conn.: Flowers & Company, 1855), 99.

42. "Prohibition in Hartford," *Hartford Daily Courant* (1840–87), March 8, 1855, 2. http://search.proquest.com/docview/553109166?_accountid=46995.

43. John Newton Stearns, *Prohibition Does Prohibit, Or, Prohibition Not a Failure* (New York: National Temperance Society & Publication House, 1875), 24.

44. *Cyclopaedia of Temperance and Prohibition*, 127.

45. Stearns, *Prohibition Does Prohibit*, 25.

46. Walter W. Scott, ed., *A Handbook for the Aggressive Temperance People of the United States*, rarebooksclub.com, 2012, 43.

47. Okrent, *Last Call*, 105.

48. Albert Edward Van Dusen, *Connecticut* (New York: Random House, 1961), 282.

49. Deets Pickett, Clarence True Wilson, and Ernest Dailey Smith, *The Cyclopedia of Temperance, Prohibition and Morals* (New York: Methodist Book Concern, 1917), 59.

50. *American Prohibition Year Book* (Lincoln Temperance Press, 1908), 44. https://books.google.com/books.

51. "City Health Department Credits Prohibition for Decrease in Death Rate," *Hartford Courant* (1887–1922), November 28, 1920, 1. http://search.proquest.com/docview/556864730?_accountid=46995.

52. "Drunks Jailed Prove Prohibition Failure, Say County Officials," *Hartford Courant* (1887–1922), December 3, 1920, 10. http://search.proquest.com/docview/556882263?_accountid=46995.

53. "Unintended Consequences," pbs.org, 2011. www.pbs.org/kenburns/prohibition/unintended-consequences/.

54. "Prohibition Failure in City of Hartford, Police Board Agrees," *Hartford Courant* (1887–1922), November 14, 1922. http://search.proquest.com/docview/557126871?_accountid=46995.

55. Karen M. Hess, Christine Hess Orthmann, and Henry Lim Cho, *Introduction to Law Enforcement and Criminal Justice* (Boston: Cengage Learning, 2014), 30.

56. Lisa McGirr, *The War on Alcohol: Prohibition and the Rise of the American State* (New York: W. W. Norton, 2015), xix.

57. Michael Newton, *The Encyclopedia of Serial Killers* (New York: Facts on File, 2006), 4.

58. Municipal Register of the City of Hartford, October 28, 1918, 460.

59. Will Siss, *Connecticut Beer: A History of Nutmeg State Brewing* (Mount Pleasant, S.C.: Arcadia, 2015), 21–22.

60. Mike Messina, "Diamonds of the Past: Hartford's Lost Ball Parks." http://connecticuthistory.org/diamonds-of-the-past-hartfords-lost-ball-parks/, retrieved March 20, 2016.

61. "To Start Factory League," *Hartford Courant* (1887–1922), June 2, 1904, 2. http://search.proquest.com/docview/555228659?_accountid=46995.

62. "Factory League," *Hartford Courant* (1887–1922), May 17, 1905, 2. http://search.proquest.com/docview/555300567?_accountid=46995.

63. "A Plea for Quiet," *Hartford Courant* (1887–1922), August 5, 1901, 7. http://search.proquest.com/docview/555085268?_accountid=46995.

64. "No Sunday Baseball," *Hartford Courant* (1887–1922), August 19, 1901, 7. http://search.proquest.com/docview/555001954?_accountid=46995.

65. "Sunday Baseball," *Hartford Courant* (1887–1922), August 10, 1901, 4. http://search.proquest.com/docview/555081279?_accountid=46995.

66. "Sporting Gossip," *Hartford Courant* (1887–1922), October 6, 1908, 13. http://search.proquest.com/docview/555584810?_accountid=46995.

67. "Tiger Cadets Play a Tie," *Hartford Courant* (1887–1922), November 1, 1909, 10. http://search.proquest.com/docview/555677595?_accountid =46995.

68. Jack Dwyer, "Letter from Carlisles," *Hartford Courant* (1887–1922), October 10, 1912, 16. http://search.proquest.com/docview/555943843 ?_accountid=46995.

69. "Rev. R. B. Ogilby Is Named to Succeed Dr. Flavel S. Luther," *Hartford Courant* (1887–1922), April 25, 1920, 1. http://search.proquest.com /docview/556797775?_accountid=46995.

70. "All Frog Hollow Gives Rousing Reception to Its Idol, 'Spud' Drew," *Hartford Courant* (1887–1922), November 18, 1920, 16. http://search.pro quest.com/docview/556866153?_accountid=46995.

71. David R. Woodward, *World War I Almanac* (New York: Infobase, 2009), 232.

72. "Russell Gives Directions for Saving Coal," *Hartford Courant* (1887–1922), October 8, 1918, 5. http://search.proquest.com/docview/556616961 ?_accountid=46995.

73. "Furnaces in Discard," *Hartford Courant* (1887–1922), January 27, 1918, 11. http://search.proquest.com/docview/556541150?_accountid=46995.

74. Maurine Weiner Greenwald, *Women, War, and Work: The Impact of World War I on Women Workers in the United States* (Ithaca, N.Y.: Cornell University Press, 1990), Preface.

75. "1920 Eventful Period in History of Connecticut's Capital City," *Hartford Courant* (1887–1922), December 31, 1920, 10. http://search.proquest .com/docview/556872039?_accountid=46995.

76. Cravens, *Great Depression*, 56.

77. Peter Tuckel, Kurt Schlichting, and Richard Maisel, "Social, Economic, and Residential Diversity within Hartford's African American Community at the Beginning of the Great Migration," *Journal of Black Studies* 37, no. 5 (May 2007): 715.

78. Robert Haws, *The Age of Segregation: Race Relations in the South, 1890–1945* (Jackson: University Press of Mississippi, 1978), 92.

79. Sarajane Cedrone, "Southern Blacks Transform Connecticut." http://ctexplored.org/southern-blacks-transform-connecticut/, retrieved April 10, 2016.

80. Roger Bruns, *Martin Luther King, Jr.: A Biography* (Santa Barbara, Calif.: Greenwood, 2006), 10.

81. Stone, *African American Connecticut*, 217.

82. Philip J. Wood, *Southern Capitalism: The Political Economy of North Carolina, 1880–1980* (Durham, N.C.: Duke University Press, 1976), 174.

83. Jim Powell, "How Did Rich Connecticut Morph into One of America's Worst-Performing Economies?" *Forbes*, August 1, 2013. www .forbes.com/sites/jimpowell/2013/08/01/how-did-rich-connecticut-morph -into-one-of-americas-worst-performing-economies/#1416f471270e.

84. Carolyn C. Jones, "Split Income and Separate Spheres: Tax Law and Gender Roles in the 1940s," *Law and History Review* 6, no. 2 (1988): 259–310, 263. doi: 10.2307/743685.

85. Maureen Honey, *Creating Rosie the Riveter: Class, Gender, and Propaganda during World War II* (Amherst: University of Massachusetts Press, 1985), 176.

86. Jones, "Split Income and Separate Spheres," 264.

87. Sherrie A. Kossoudji and Laura J. Dresser, "Working Class Rosies: Women Industrial Workers during World War II," *Journal of Economic History* 52, no. 2 (1992): 431–46, 432. www.jstor.org/stable/2123119.

88. Sara Harrington, "Women's Work: Domestic Labor in American World War II Posters," *Art Documentation: Journal of the Art Libraries Society of North America* 22, no. 2 (2003): 41–44, 43. www.jstor.org/stable /27949264.

89. Jones, "Split Income and Separate Spheres," 263.

90. "Women in Industry," *Monthly Labor Review* 57, no. 4 (1943): 723–28, 723. www.jstor.org/stable/41817253.

91. Martin H. Blatt and Martha K. Norkunas, *Work, Recreation, and Culture: Essays in American Labor History* (New York: Routledge, 2013), 13.

92. Susan E. Riley, "Caring for Rosie's Children: Federal Child Care

Policies in the World War II Era," *Polity* 26, no. 4 (1994): 655–75, 656. doi: 10.2307/3235099.

93. Claudia D. Goldin, "The Role of World War II in the Rise of Women's Employment," *American Economic Review* 8, no. 4 (1991): 741–56, 741. www.jstor.org/stable/2006640.

94. Doris Weatherford, *American Women during World War II* (New York: Routledge, 2009), 405.

95. Valerie K. Oppenheimer, "The Interaction of Demand and Supply and Its Effect on the Female Labour Force in the United States," *Population Studies* 21, no. 3 (1967): 239–59, 239. doi: 10.2307/2173145.

96. Ibid.

6. Each Man and Woman

1. "The Fugitive Slave Case," *Hartford Daily Courant* (1840–87), May 30, 1854, 2. http://search.proquest.com/docview/553075367?_accountid=46995.

2. George W. Callahan, *Minutemen of 61* (Bloomington, Ind.: Trafford, 2011), 19.

3. "The Connecticut Personal Liberty Bill," *Hartford Daily Courant* (1840–87), November 27, 1860, 2. http://search.proquest.com/docview/553323411?_accountid=46995.

4. David E. Swift, *Black Prophets of Justice: Activist Clergy before the Civil War* (Baton Rouge: Louisiana State University Press, 1989), 206.

5. Ibid., 212.

6. *American Anti-Slavery Almanac*, 1839, 35.

7. James W. C. Pennington, *The Fugitive Blacksmith; Or, Events in the History of James W. C. Pennington, Formerly a Slave in the State of Maryland, United States* (London: C. Gilpin, 1849), 61.

8. John Hooker, *Reminiscences of a Long Life: With a Few Articles on Moral and Social Subjects of Present Interest* (Hartford, Conn.: Belknap & Warfield, 1899), 40.

9. Christopher Webber, *American to the Backbone: The Life of James Pennington, the Fugitive Slave Who Became One of the First Abolitionists* (New York: Pegasus Books, 2011), 383.

10. Jackson Turner Main, *Society and Economy in Colonial Connecticut* (Princeton, N.J.: Princeton University Press, 2014), 355.

11. William F. Sullivan Jr., "Born to Be Hanged: What Runaway Apprentice Advertisements Reveal about Connecticut's Master Craftsmen in the Early Republic." http://runawayct.org/born-to-be-hanged, retrieved January 25, 2016.

12. Antonio T. Bly, *Escaping Bondage: A Documentary History of Runaway Slaves in Eighteenth Century New England, 1700–1789* (Lanham, Md.: Lexington Books, 2010), 230.

13. Graham Russell Hodges and Alan Edward Brown, *Pretends to Be Free: Runaway Slave Advertisements from Colonial and Revolutionary New York and New Jersey* (Florence, Ky.: Taylor & Francis, 1994), 47.

14. Matthew Warshauer, *Connecticut in the American Civil War: Slavery, Sacrifice, and Survival* (Middletown, Conn.: Wesleyan University Press, 2011), 2.

15. Kathleena Lucille Roark, *Acting American in the Age of Abolition: Transatlantic Black American Celebrity and the Rise of Yankee Theatre, 1787–1827* (Ann Arbor, Mich.: Proquest, 2007), 47.

16. "Editorial Article 1—No Title," *Hartford Daily Courant* (1840–87), February 8, 1860, 2. http://search.proquest.com/docview/553311033?_accountid=46995.

17. Anne Farrow, Joel Lang, and Jenifer Frank, *Complicity: How the North Promoted, Prolonged, and Profited from Slavery* (New York: Random House, 2007), 159.

18. David Menschel, "Abolition without Deliverance: The Law of Connecticut Slavery 1784–1848," *Yale Law Journal* 111, no. 1 (October 2001). www.yalelawjournal.org/note/abolition-without-deliverance-the-law-of-connecticut-slavery-1784–1848.

19. A. Lincoln, "Message of the President," *Hartford Daily Courant* (1840–87), March 7, 1862. http://search.proquest.com/docview/553364198?_accountid=46995.

20. "The Negro Vote in Old New York," *Political Science Quarterly* 4–38 (1917): 254.

21. Noah Webster, "Effects of Slavery on Morals and Industry." http://

quod.lib.umich.edu/e/evans/N20179.0001.001/1: 4? rgn=div1; view
=fulltext, retrieved March 15, 2016.

22. Joanne Pope Melish, *Disowning Slavery: Gradual Emancipation and
"Race" in New England* (Ithaca, N.Y.: Cornell University Press, 1998), 84.

23. Willis I. Twitchell, *Hartford in History: A Series of Papers by Resident
Authors* (Hartford, Conn.: Plimpton Manufacturing Co., 1907), 94.

24. Ibid.

25. "Constitution of the Hartford Auxiliary Colonization Society,
Together with an Address to the Public" (Hartford, Conn.: Lincoln &
Stone, 1819), 7–8. http://scua.library.umass.edu/digital/antislavery/154
.pdf.

26. "Annual Meeting," *Connecticut Courant* (1791–1837), June 15, 1830, 2.
http://search.proquest.com/docview/548524977?_accountid=46995.

27. *Frederick Douglass: Selected Speeches and Writings* (Chicago: Chicago
Review Press, 2000), 125.

28. Warshauer, *Connecticut in the American Civil War*, 4.

29. Allen Carden, *Freedom's Delay: America's Struggle for Emancipation,
1776–1865* (Knoxville: University of Tennessee Press, 2014), 52.

30. Charles S. Johnson, "The Negro Population of Hartford,
Connecticut" (New York: National Urban League, 1921). http://digital
repository.trincoll.edu/cssp_archives/15/.

31. John David Smith, *Lincoln and the U.S. Colored Troops* (Carbondale:
Southern Illinois University Press, 2013), 28.

32. Christine Knauer, *Let Us Fight As Free Men: Black Soldiers and Civil
Rights* (Philadelphia: University of Pennsylvania Press, 2014). 7.

33. "Classified Ad 3—No Title," *Hartford Daily Courant* (1840–87), October 11, 1862, 3. http://search.proquest.com/docview/553405352?_accountid
=46995.

34. Dione Longley and Buck Zaidel, *Heroes for All Time: Connecticut
Civil War Soldiers Tell Their Stories* (Middletown, Conn.: Wesleyan
University Press, 2015), 101.

35. Smith, *Lincoln and the U.S. Colored Troops*, 75.

36. Todd Jones, "29th Regiment Connecticut Volunteers Fought More
Than One War." http://connecticuthistory.org/the-29th-regiment-connect

icut-volunteers-fought-more-than-one-war/, retrieved March 12, 2016.

37. Elizabeth J. Normen, ed., *African American Connecticut Explored* (Middletown, Conn.: Wesleyan University Press, 2014) 80.

38. "The President and the Negroes," *Hartford Daily Courant* (1840–87), October 12, 1865, 2. http://search.proquest.com/docview/553449205 ?_accountid=46995.

39. J. H. Almy, "The 29th Regiment," *Hartford Daily Courant* (1840–87), November 23, 1865, 2. http://search.proquest.com/docview/553446952 ?_accountid=46995.

40. "Reception of Colored Regiments," *Hartford Daily Courant* (1840–87), November 25, 1865, 2. http://search.proquest.com/docview /553497824?_accountid=46995.

41. Ibid, 168.

42. "Fifteenth Amendment Celebration," *Hartford Daily Courant* (1840–87), August 4, 1871. http://search.proquest.com/docview/553694696 ?_accountid=46995.

43. Kathleen Housley, "Yours for the Oppressed: The Life of Jehiel C. Beman," *Journal of Negro History* 771 (1992): 17–29. www.jstor.org.unh -proxy01.newhaven.edu: 2048/stable/3031524? seq=1#page_scan_tab _contents.

44. William J. Collins, "Race, Roosevelt, and Wartime Production: Fair Employment in World War II Labor Markets," *American Economic Review* 91, no. 1 (2001): 272–86. www.jstor.org/stable/2677909.

45. Leslie M. Swann, "African American Women in the World War II Defense Industry," Order No. 3151038, Temple University, 2004. http:// unh-proxy01.newhaven.edu: 2048/login? url=http://search.proquest.com /docview/305133804?_accountid=8117.

46. Ibid.

47. James N. Gregory, *The Southern Diaspora: How the Great Migrations of Black and White Southerners Transformed America* (Chapel Hill: University of North Carolina Press, 2006), 65.

48. Isabel Wilkerson, *The Warmth of Other Suns: The Epic Story of America's Great Migration* (New York: Knopf Doubleday, 2010), 6.

49. Alferdteen Harrison, *Black Exodus: The Great Migration from the American South* (Jackson: University Press of Mississippi, 1992), 38.

50. Wilkerson, *Warmth of Other Suns*, 7.

51. Tuckel, Schlichting, and Maisel, "Social, Economic, and Residential Diversity," 715.

52. W. M. E. "The Russo-Jewish Immigrants," *Hartford Daily Courant* (1840–87), June 27, 1882, 1. http://search.proquest.com/docview /554191311?_accountid=46995.

53. Maynard Shipley, "Effects of Immigration on Homicide in American Cities," *Popular Science Monthly*, August 1906, 168. https://books.google. com/books?

54. "Immigrants Win School Debate," *Hartford Courant* (1887–1922), June 1, 1907, 13. http://search.proquest.com/docview/555474697?_account id=46995.

55. Kathleen R. Arnold, ed., *Contemporary Immigration in America: A State-by-State Encyclopedia* (Santa Barbara, Calif.: ABC-CLIO, 2015), 115.

56. "The Story of Connecticut's Italians." http://wethersfieldhistory.org /articles-from-the-community/the_story_of_connecticuts_italians/, retrieved March 17, 2016.

7. Growing Weary and Mistrustful

1. "The Cholera," *Hartford Daily Courant* (1840–87), August 8, 1849, 2. http://search.proquest.com/docview/552876653?_accountid=46995.

2. *Bulletin of the Johns Hopkins University* 31 (1920): 285.

3. "The Cholera," *Hartford Daily Courant* (1840–87), April 26, 1854. http://search.proquest.com/docview/553072093?_accountid=46995.

4. Timothy A. Hasci, *Second Home: Orphan Asylums and Poor Families in America* (Cambridge, Mass.: Harvard University Press, 1997), 11.

5. Trumbull, *Memorial History of Hartford County*, 553.

6. Wm. Goodwin, *Hartford Daily Courant* (1840–87), December 11, 1849, 2. Retrieved from proquest.com.

7. Edward Warren Capen, *The Historical Development of the Poor Law of Connecticut* (New York: Columbia University Press, 1905), 263.

8. They Are Innately Capable

1. Richard Severo, "John Gregory Dunne, Novelist, Screenwriter and Observer of Hollywood, Is Dead at 71," *New York Times*, January 1, 2004. www.nytimes.com/2004/01/01/arts/john-gregory-dunne-novelist-screenwriter-and-observer-of-hollywood-is-dead-at-71.html?_r=0.

2. John Gregory Dunne, *The Art of Making Magazines: On Being an Editor and Other Views from the Industry*, edited by Victor Navasky and Evan Cornog (New York: Columbia University Press, 2012), 7.

3. Ibid.

4. "Struck with a Cleaver," *Hartford Courant* (1887–1922), January 29, 1896, 6. http://search.proquest.com/docview/554652142?_account id=46995.

5. "Park Street Trust Opens Its Doors," *Hartford Courant* (1887–1922), April 4, 1920, 16. http://search.proquest.com/docview/556803417?_accountid=46995.

6. Arnold, *Contemporary Immigration in America*, 121.

7. John Ranelagh, *A Short History of Ireland* (Cambridge, U.K.: Cambridge University Press, 2012), 111.

8. Jennifer Herman, *Connecticut Encyclopedia* (New York: State Historical Publications, 2008), 70.

9. Jay P. Dolan, *Irish Americans: A History* (London: Bloomsbury USA, 2010), x.

10. Ibid.

11. Colin Haydon, *Anti-Catholicism in Eighteenth-Century England, c. 1714–80: A Political and Social Study* (Manchester, U.K.: Manchester University Press, 1993), 22.

12. Chip Berlet and Matthew Nemiroff Lyons, *Right-Wing Populism in America: Too Close for Comfort* (New York: Guilford Press, 2000), 47.

13. Ibid.

14. O'Donnell and Michaud, *Diocese of Hartford*, 26.

15. Stephen Lassonde, *Learning to Forget: Schooling and Family Life in New Haven's Working Class, 1870–1940* (New Haven, Conn.: Yale University Press, 2008), 15.

16. *An Account of the Farmington Canal Company: Of the Hampshire and Hamden Canal Company; And of the New Haven and Northampton Company, Till the Suspension of Its Canal in 1847* (New Haven, Conn.: T. J. Stafford, 1850), 21.

17. Lassonde, *Learning to Forget*, 15.

18. Michael V. Uschan, *Irish Americans* (New York: Gareth Stevens, 2006), 25.

19. Trumbull, *Memorial History of Hartford County*, 26.

20. Dolan, *Irish Americans*, 137.

21. Andrew Walsh and Mark Silk, *Religion and Public Life in New England: Steady Habits, Changing Slowly* (Lanham, Md.: Roman Altamira, 2004), 43.

22. Ibid., 44.

23. William E. Gienapp, *The Origins of the Republican Party, 1852–1856* (Oxford, U.K.: Oxford University Press, 1988), 275.

24. "Late 19th-Century Immigration in Connecticut." http://connecticut history.org/late-19th-century-immigration-in-connecticut/, retrieved December 27, 2015.

25. "Democratic War on Irish Voters," *Hartford Daily Courant* (1840–87), March 31, 1870, 2. https://search-proquest-com.unh-proxy01 .newhaven.edu/hnphartfordcourant/docview/553708829/604343CC 80E45DCPQ/1?accountid=8117.

26. "The Irish People Who Live in Hartford: From Colonial Times They Have Played an Important Part in the Affairs of the City and State— More People of Irish Blood in Hartford Than Any Other—No Other Race Holds So Many Political Offices—History of Religious Activities," *Hartford Courant* (1887–1922), February 13, 1916, X1.

27. George J. Borjas and Richard B. Freeman, *Immigration and the Work Force: Economic Consequences for the United States and Source Areas* (Chicago: University of Chicago Press, 2007), 190.

28. José Ramón Sánchez, *Boricua Power: A Political History of Puerto Ricans in the United States* (New York: New York University Press, 2007), 50.

29. Walsh, "Hartford: A Global History," 35.

30. Richard Worth, *1950s to 1960s* (Singapore: Marshall Cavendish, 2009), 50.

31. Donald Joseph Smyth, "Institutional Growth in a Residential Area: A Case Study of Hartford Hospital" (thesis, University of Rhode Island, 1979). http://digitalcommons.uri.edu/cgi/viewcontent.cgi?_article =1525&context=theses.

32. "Hartford, Connecticut General Development Plan, Background Studies, Part 1" (Hartford, Conn.: Parkins, Rogers & Associates, 1964), 34.

33. Sacks, "Suburbanization and Racial/Ethnic Divide," 5.

34. Radcliffe, *Charter Oak Terrace*, 1.

35. Evelyn Nieves, "A Violent Battle of Wills Besieges Hartford," *New York Times*, December 25, 1994. www.nytimes.com/1994/12/25/nyregion /a-violent-battle-of-wills-besieges-hartford.html? pagewanted=all.

36. César J. Ayala, "The Decline of the Plantation Economy and the Puerto Rican Migration of the 1950s," *Latino Studies Journal* 7, no. 1 (Winter 1996): 61–90. http://lcw.lehman.edu/lehman/depts /latinampuertorican/latinoweb/PuertoRico/ayalamigration.pdf.

37. Cruz, *Identity and Power*, 92.

38. "Maria Sánchez, State Representative and Community Advocate." http://connecticuthistory.org/maria-sanchez-state-representative-and -community-advocate/, retrieved March 18, 2016.

39. Cruz, *Identity and Power*, 163.

40. José E. Cruz, "A Decade of Change: Puerto Rican Politics in Connecticut, 1969–1979," 69. www.trincoll.edu/UrbanGlobal/CUGS /Faculty/research/Documents/A% 20Decade% 20of% 20Change % 20Puerto% 20Rican% 20Politics% 20in% 20Hartford, %20Connecticut, %201969–1979.pdf, retrieved July 22, 2016.

41. *Courant* staff writers E. M. Weiss and Matt Burgard contributed to this story. "Call Him 'Senor Alcalde'; Hartford: Perez Sweeps to Overwhelming Victory as First Hispanic Mayor," *Hartford Courant*, November 7, 2001. http://search.proquest.com/docview/256410972? _accountid=46995.

42. Kenneth J. Neubeck and Richard E. Ratcliff, "Urban Democracy and the Power of Corporate Capital: Struggles over Downtown Growth and

Neighborhood Stagnation in Hartford, Connecticut," in *Business Elites and Urban Development: Case Studies and Critical Perspectives*, edited by Scott Cummings (Albany: State University of New York Press, 1988), 306.

43. Ibid.

44. James R. Bowers and Wilbur C. Rich, *Governing Middle-Sized Cities: Studies in Mayoral Leadership* (Boulder, Colo.: Lynne Rienner, 2000), 37.

45. Donald F. Fenton, "Politics of Change: Mayor vs. Manager," March 31, 2016. http://ctexplored.org/politics-of-change-mayor-vs-manager/.

46. "Hartford No Longer a 'Company Town,'" *Hartford Courant*, August 28, 1994, A13. http://search.proquest.com/docview/255471818?_accountid =46995.

47. David Radcliffe, *People's History: The Story of Hartford Areas Rally Together* (Hartford, Conn.: HART, 1995), 28.

48. Ibid., 69.

49. Ibid., 177.

50. Suzanne Lis, "White Flight in Hartford County, CT: 1950–2010," Tufts University, "Intro to GIS," 2012. http://sites.tufts.edu/gis/files/2013 /11/Lis_Suzanne.pdf.

51. Sacks, "Suburbanization and Racial/Ethnic Divide," 1.

52. M. Swift and *Courant* staff writer, "Hartford Lets the Good Times Go; Value of a Bustling Suburb's Taxable Property Tops City's," *Hartford Courant*, July 6, 2000. http://search.proquest.com/docview/256311382 ?_accountid=46995.

53. Mike Swift and *Courant* staff writer, "Hartford Lets the Good Times Go; Value of a Bustling Suburb's Taxable Property Tops City's," *Hartford Courant*, July 6, 2000, A1. http://search.proquest.com/docview/256311382 ?_accountid=46995.

54. Gregory Seay and *Courant* staff writer, "Hartford Fish Market Plans Move to Suburbs," *Hartford Courant*, March 8, 1994, D1. http://search .proquest.com/docview/255371803?_accountid=46995.

55. Johnny Mason and *Courant* staff writer, "Fire Destroys Former City Fish Market; No One Injured in Sunday Afternoon Blaze at Bostonian Fishery Building," *Hartford Courant*, November 13, 2000, B1. http://search .proquest.com/docview/256309639?_accountid=46995.

56. Christian Montès, *American Capitals: A Historical Geography* (Chicago: University of Chicago Press, 2014), 219.

57. www.prisoncensorship.info/archive/etext/mn/mn188/alkqn.txt, retrieved March 11, 2016.

58. Ibid.

59. David J. Leonard and Carmen R. Lugo-Lugo, *Latin History and Culture: An Encyclopedia* (New York: Routledge, 2015), 447.

60. http://thehoodup.com/board/viewtopic.php?t=43773#.Vt_-qp MrIzY.

61. Lucas Rivera, "The Anatomy of a King," *Vibe* 4, no. 7 (September 1996): 168.

62. Merrill Singer, *The Face of Social Suffering: The Life History of a Street Drug Addict* (Long Grove, Ill.: Waveland Press, 2005), 83.

63. "Family Values: The Gangster Version," *Harper's Magazine*, April 1995, 18.

64. Ibid.

65. Ibid.

66. Albert DiChiara and Russell Chabot, "Gangs and the Contemporary Urban Struggle: An Unappreciated Aspect of Gangs," in *Gangs in Society: Alternative Perspectives*, edited by Louis Kontos, David C. Brotherton, and Luis Barrios (New York: Columbia University Press, 2012), 76.

67. Ibid., 80.

68. Personal interview with the author, June 2014.

69. Matthew Kauffman, "Many Embrace Operation Liberty Despite Methods," *Hartford Courant*, September 30, 1993. http://articles.courant.com/1993–09–30/news/0000004129_1_gang-members-latin-kings-two-local-gangs.

70. Jenna Carlesso, "Twenty Years Ago, Shooting Death Drove City's War on Gang Violence," *Hartford Courant*, October 28, 2014. www.courant.com/courant-250/moments-in-history/hc-250-hartford-gangs-20141027-story.html.

71. Ibid.

72. Elizabeth Hinton, *From the War on Poverty to the War on Crime* (Cambridge, Mass.: Harvard University Press, 2016), 321.

73. Mona Chalabi, "The 'War on Drugs' in Numbers: A Systemic Failure of Policy," *Guardian*, April 19, 2016. www.theguardian.com/world/2 016 /apr/19/war-on-drugs-statistics-systematic-policy-failure-united-nations.

74. Johnny Mason Jr. and *Courant* Correspondent, "Off the Street Frog Hollow Parents Wanted a Place for Their Kids, So They Fought For and Got the $5 Million Pope Park Recreational Center," *Hartford Courant*, February 23, 1997. http://search.proquest.com/docview/255811463? _accountid=46995.

75. "Frog Hollow and Redlining," *Hartford Courant*, January 8, 1998, A14. http://search.proquest.com/docview/255963511?_accountid=46995.

76. Stacey Stowe, "Latest Merger Makes It Clearer Than Ever: Hartford Is No Longer the Insurance Capital," *New York Times*, November 21, 2003. www.nytimes.com/2003/11/21/nyregion/latest-merger-makes-it-clearer -than-ever-hartford-no-longer-insurance-capital.html.

77. Bruce D. Wundt, "Defense Cuts: What Might Connecticut Expect on the Manufacturing Employment Front," *New England Journal of Public Policy* 7, no. 2 (1991): article 8, 105.

78. Ibid., 106.

79. "Fiscal Cliff Just the Beginning for State's Defense Industries," Connecticut Business and Industry Association. www.cbia.com/news /inside-the-capitol/fiscal-cliff-just-the-beginning-for-states-defense -industries/, retrieved March 11, 2016.

80. Tom Condon, "The Church Frog Hollow Nourished," *Hartford Courant*, September 7, 2000, A3. http://search.proquest.com/docview /256302602?_accountid=46995.

81. www.hartfordschools.org/come-to-the-latino-studies-academy-at -burns-school-rededication/, retrieved March 17, 2017.

9. *Regardless of Fortuitous Circumstances*

1. Warren R. Copeland, *Doing Justice in Our Cities: Lessons in Public Policy from America's Heartland* (Louisville, Ky.: Westminster John Knox Press, 2009), 19.

2. Bruce Katz, *Reflections on Regionalism* (Washington, D.C.: Brookings Institution Press, 2001), 86.

3. David Rusk, "'Inelastic' Cities Need Help from the Suburbs," *Baltimore Sun*, June 8, 1993. http://articles.baltimoresun.com/1993–06–08 /news/1993159116_1_elastic-city-limits-inner-city.

4. Ibid.

5. Ibid.

6. Vinny Vella, "From Lyric to Library? City's Plan to Replace Old Theatre Hits Opposition," *Hartford Courant*, February 19, 2017, B-1.

7. https://wallethub.com/edu/best-state-capitals/19030/#main -findings, retrieved 3/14/17.

8. www.metrohartfordprogresspoints.org/downloads/Metro _Hartford_Progress_Points_2014.pdf, retrieved May 28, 2016.

9. Ray Oldenburg, *The Great, Good Place: Cafes, Coffee Shops, Bookstores, Bars, Hair Salons and Other Hangouts at the Heart of a Community* (Cambridge, Mass.: Da Capo Press, 1989), x.

Index

SUSAN CAMPBELL is the author most recently of *Tempest-Tossed: The Spirit of Isabella Beecher Hooker.* She has appeared on CBS *News Sunday Morning,* the BBC, and WNPR. Her column about the March 1998 shootings in Newington, Connecticut, was part of the *Hartford Courant's* Pulitzer Prize–winning coverage of the tragedy.